GOD'S WORD ON HEALING

Scripture Verses on Healing and God's Promises With Miracle Testimonies

The following verses have been humbly assembled to His glory by Nancy Insley

His Healing Touch
Portland, Oregon, USA

"Heal the sick, cleanse the lepers, raise the dead, cast out devils."
Matthew 10:8a

Out of reverence to our God and King, I have capitalized references to God, His Son, and the Holy Spirit. In both versions, I have added quotation marks to quotes (something neither of these versions do), as it is less confusing to the reader. A verse standing alone in quotes indicates Jesus' words. Parentheses ( ) before the text clarify its background. When verses in The Amplified Bible version have words within parentheses, it signifies additional meanings which are included in the original word or phrase, while brackets [ ] contain justified clarifying words. Statements in *italics* and set off in italicized brackets *{ }* are my thoughts. Underlining, bold text and words in all capital letters have been added for emphasis.

For additional copies, teachings or to request a speaking engagement, please write to:

HisHealingTouchMinistry@msn.com

Fourth Revision: December, 2010
Third Revision: September, 2005
Second Revision: July, 2005
First Revision: June, 1999
First Printing: October, 1997

TABLE OF CONTENTS

A TESTIMONY OF HEALING

At the age of 15, I jumped into a swimming pool and severely injured my back. It never healed properly; and in the years following the accident, I was forced to wear back braces, sit on a special chair, and undergo continual physical therapy with a variety of treatments. Standing, walking, sitting and lying down all brought misery. When I walked, I had to drag my bad leg behind me, particularly when going up stairs. The extreme pain made it a challenge to focus my  mind, so I eventually had to quit my job as a systems engineer for IBM. Sleep was rare and shallow, because no position was tolerable. Three times the surgeons operated on my spinal column, but nothing helped to relieve the pain. In fact, the pain only worsened until I was primarily confined to my bed for five years, with no hope of improvement.

During most of this time, I lived in Germany. Once, when I flew home for my sister's wedding, sitting for the long, 16-hour flight was impossible, so I had to lie across the laps of my traveling companions! When I finally returned to the United States to live, the airline put me in a special metal carrier which they suspended from the wall of the plane.

The doctors did all they could to help me, but the damage caused by the original injury left bone points sticking into three nerve roots that caused a constant irritation the doctors were unable to relieve. The damaged nerves caused deadness in my leg that could not be restored. The doctors were unable to help me any further and said that I would have to resign myself to a life in bed, never holding down a job nor bearing children.

After suffering 17½ years of that acute, incapacitating pain, I attended a meeting where the pastor understood the Word of God regarding healing. He prayed, laying his hand on me, and I was marvelously healed!

Not surprisingly, the subject of healing suddenly piqued my interest, and God began to teach me from His Word. I was amazed at what had been in Scripture all along–things of which I had previously never really taken note. The Lord had me begin studying in the Gospels, and the first thing I noticed was the strong connection between faith and healing. I knew I would have to understand and grow in faith in order to walk in health.

Applying what I was learning totally changed my family's lives. Since that time, we have experienced numerous healings and miracles. In different accidents, both our children could have died or been maimed for life. In fact, our son was born with a fatal heart defect that the doctors could do nothing about. After prayer, we took him back to the heart specialist when he was just a few days old and learned that his heart had been totally healed! I, too, have been healed of many sicknesses, including a large tumor, kidney stones, a presumably broken ankle, a twisted ankle and migraine headaches.

In recent years, I have been teaching on healing and the love of God to individuals, groups, pastors and leaders, both in the United States and around the world. I have had the awesome privilege of seeing thousands of people instantly healed, as they grow in faith and understanding. Individuals leave the meetings changed, expectant, excited and more in love with God than ever before. God is good, His Word is true, and He is faithful to His Word! God is the Healer, and *His Healing Touch* is still for today. I pray that you will also experience God's love and trust Him for your healing.

Nancy Insley

GOD'S WORD ON HEALING

The Holy Spirit led me to go through the New Testament, searching out verses that refer to the close connection between faith and healing. Furthermore, I was finding many references in the Old Testament which clearly made this same association. In the process of this study, the importance of the words which we speak became quite evident to me. My eyes were opened to the correlation between faith, words, our authority in Christ, and healing, as I hope yours will be, also.

God said, "My people are destroyed for lack of knowledge" (Hosea 4:6a). I "desire that ye might be filled with the knowledge of His will in all wisdom and spiritual understanding" (Colossians 1:9). His "Word is a lamp unto my feet, and a light unto my path" (Psalm 119:105). "For the commandment is a lamp; and the law is light; and reproofs of instruction are the way of **life**" (Proverbs 6:23). "The statutes of the LORD are right, rejoicing the heart: the commandment of the LORD is pure, enlightening the eyes" (Psalm 19: 8). Let your eyes be enlightened, and let your heart rejoice. "Prove all things; hold fast that which is good" (1 Thessalonians 5:21). "Know *and* understand that it is [really] the people [who live] by faith who are [the true] sons of Abraham" (Galatians 3:7 AMP).

Jesus healed, cast out demons, and more. If sickness were from God, then Jesus would have been undoing God's work and working against God's will. That would not be consistent with the character of Jesus: "And He that sent Me is with Me: the Father hath not left Me alone; for I do always those things that please Him" (John 8:29). "...I do nothing of Myself (of My own accord or on My own authority), but I say [exactly] what My Father has taught Me. Anyone who has seen Me has seen the Father..." (John 8:28b AMP and John 14:9b AMP). "...The Son can do nothing of Himself, but what He seeth the Father do: for what things soever He doeth, these also doeth the Son likewise" (John 5:19).

Why do you suppose there is no sickness in heaven? Because sickness is not from God! Jesus never made anyone sick; He only healed. He never said He would place a sickness or injury on someone, so that that person might draw closer to Him. Jesus says, "If ye then, being evil, know how to give good gifts unto your children, how much more shall your Father which is in heaven give good things to them that ask Him?" (Matthew 7:11). Sickness is not a good gift, and parents do not desire to give their children illnesses, so why would the Father? "Blessed be the God and Father of our Lord Jesus Christ, who hath blessed us with **all** spiritual blessings in heavenly places in Christ" (Ephesians 1:3).

Could it be: "Ye have not, because ye ask not" (James 4:2)? We used to follow "the course of this world, according to the prince of the power of the air, the spirit that now worketh in the children of disobedience" (Ephesians 2:2), "but God—so rich is He in His mercy!... He made us alive together in fellowship *and* in union with

Christ..." (Ephesians 2:4, 5 AMP). Why should we keep listening to the evil one instead of the Words of our Savior? "Teach me Thy Way, O LORD, and lead me in a plain path" (Psalm 27:11).

The Lord is trustworthy and will keep all of His promises. "As for God, His way is perfect! The Word of the Lord is tested *and* tried..." (Psalm 18:30 AMP). The world has taught us to speak many words of the devil without us realizing it. We need to become aware of the words we are speaking. Our words should agree with God's Word and be ones that confess God's promises to us. A great number of verses talk about putting a hand on the mouth. This is to remind us to avoid speaking unworthy, evil and worthless words.

Everyone gets what he expects and speaks: If you are speaking sickness (and thereby confirming the works of the devil), then you confirm and receive sickness. If, instead, you speak according to God's will, you can stand on His promises and receive them: "Truly I tell you, whoever **says** to this mountain, 'Be lifted up and thrown into the sea!' and does not doubt at all in his heart but believes that what he **says** will take place, it will be done for him" (Mark 11:23 AMP). This means that you determine the direction and the quality of your life. I pray, through the reading of these Words of our Lord, that **"you will know the Truth and the Truth will make you free"** (John 8:32 RSV). "For with God nothing is ever impossible *and* no Word from God shall be **without power** *or* **impossible of fulfillment**" (Luke 1:37 AMP). Amen!

SALVATION

Healing Is a Part of Our Salvation

...there is no respect of persons (no partiality) with Him.

He has sent me to bind up *and* heal the brokenhearted, to proclaim **liberty** to the [physical and spiritual] captives and the opening of the prison *and* of the eyes to those who are **bound**.

Isaiah 61:1b AMP

"The Spirit of the Lord is upon Me, because He hath anointed Me to preach the Gospel to the poor; He hath sent Me to heal the brokenhearted, to preach deliverance to the captives, and recovering of sight to the blind, to set at liberty them that are bruised,"

Luke 4:18

(For He saith, "I have heard thee in a time accepted, and in the day of salvation have I succoured thee: behold, now is the accepted time; behold, now is the day of **salvation**.") *{"Salvation" here means "rescue or safety (physically or* *morally):--deliver,* **health**, *salvation, save, saving"* *according to Strong's word 4991, "soteria". Today is your day of health!}*

2 Corinthians 6:2

When evening came, they brought to Him many who were under the power of demons, and He drove out the spirits with a word and restored to health **all** who were **sick**. **And thus** He <u>fulfilled</u> what was spoken by the prophet Isaiah, "He Himself took [in order to carry away] our weaknesses *and* infirmities and bore away our diseases." [Isa. 53:4.] *{He <u>already</u> bore our sicknesses away for us; that is, He removed them.}*

Matthew 8:16, 17 AMP

He is despised and rejected of men; a Man of sorrows, and acquainted with grief: and we hid as it were our faces from Him; He was despised, and we esteemed Him not. Surely He <u>hath borne</u> our griefs *{lit.: sicknesses, diseases}*, and carried our sorrows *{lit.: pain, afflictions}*: yet we did esteem Him stricken, smitten of God, and afflicted. But He was wounded for our transgressions, He was bruised for our iniquities: the chastisement of our peace *{lit.: health, welfare, wholeness, prosperity, peace, rest and safety}* was upon Him; and <u>with His stripes **we are healed**</u>. *{He carried our pains and diseases <u>for</u> us. We **are** healed!}*

Isaiah 53:3-5

Then they cry unto the LORD in their trouble, and He saveth them out of their distresses. He sent His Word, and healed them, and delivered them from their destructions. *{Jesus is the Word which was sent; He has already healed us.}*

Psalm 107:19, 20

"But unto you that fear My Name shall the Sun of righteousness arise with healing in His wings..."

Malachi 4:2

Extreme Insomnia Cured

"For most of my life, I had had trouble sleeping. Staring at the ceiling for what seemed like hours at night as a child, I would listen to my mom's activities, hear her go to bed, and know when she had fallen asleep. I tried drinking warm milk, listening to relaxation tapes, counting sheep and anything else we could think of, but it did not help. As I got older, I had nights where I would not sleep for even one minute. Just a few months ago, a doctor, who was shocked at someone having so much trouble sleeping, even as a child, prescribed some sleeping pills. They worked for a while, but after a month or two, they no longer seemed to help. I was desperate for healing. Within a week after listening to the healing teaching and being prayed for, I was able to enjoy true, peaceful sleep for the first time in my life! I had no idea that one could actually dream every night. This was a real miracle! Praise God for His healing power!"—Heather

And [He] hath raised up an Horn of salvation for us...that He would grant unto us, that we being **delivered** out of the hand of our enemies might serve Him **without fear**.

Luke 1:69, 74

And it shall come to pass in that day, that his burden shall be taken away from off thy shoulder, and his yoke from off thy neck, and the yoke shall be <u>destroyed</u> because of the anointing.

Isaiah 10:27

For this <u>purpose</u> the Son of God was manifested, that He might **destroy** the works of the devil. *{The works of the devil are sickness, fear, death, frustration, lies, pain,* *disease, depression, and more. They have been destroyed that we might live free of them.}*

1 John 3:8b

"For the Son of man is <u>not come to destroy</u> men's lives, but to save them." *{To "save" them is "sozo", which also means to heal or to be made whole, to deliver, to protect and to preserve. Jesus came to save us, to heal us, to make us whole, to deliver us and to protect us. Hallelujah!}*

Luke 9:56a

"My Blood Pressure Had Been Spiking Uncontrollably"

"I was worried. My blood pressure had been spiking uncontrollably, so that I was doubling my daily dosage of medication. Not only did I take a tablet in the morning, but as I monitored my blood pressure, I found I needed to take a tablet in the evening, as well. I was having a hard time keeping the lower number (diastolic) below 80, and my average blood pressure (after two tablets per day) was around 180/90. The lower number had even just spiked to 102! I had been putting off making an appointment with my doctor to get a different medication or a higher dosage. I didn't know what else to do. I had prayed for the Lord's healing, but I had seen no changes.

"When Nancy and her husband came over for dinner the end of 2007, I mentioned this to her. She asked me excitedly, 'Well, do you want to be healed?' 'Of course!!' I told her. As we all agreed for the healing that was mine in the Lord, I felt a rejoicing in His grace and compassion; then I felt His power: a strong heaviness settled just below my breast bone. It was as if all the energy of my body had

moved to the center of my being and concentrated there. I knew that I was healed. I checked my blood pressure. It was normal (132/60)! Hallelujah! The following morning it was 130/62.

"We left for the beach the next morning, and I took my blood pressure medications and cuff with me—just in case. I praised God each time I took my blood pressure over those days. It remained completely normal without any medication. My Great Physician had healed me once again! This morning, before I sat down to write this testimony, I checked it again. It was 123/60. Not only do we receive His divine healing, but He enables us to walk in it every day. What a powerful and gracious God we serve!"—Paula

...that through death He might <u>destroy</u> him that had the power of death, that is, the devil; and <u>deliver</u> them who through fear of death were all their lifetime subject to <u>bondage</u>. *{We are no longer subject to bondage to the devil—his power has been destroyed!}*

Hebrews 2:14b, 15

To appoint unto them that mourn in Zion, to give unto them beauty for ashes, the oil of joy for mourning, the garment of praise for the <u>spirit</u> of heaviness; that they might be called trees of righteousness, the planting of the LORD, that He might be glorified.

Isaiah 61:3

"The thief (Satan) cometh not, but for to steal, and to kill, and to destroy: I am come that they might have life, and that they might have it more abundantly."

John 10:10

Giving thanks unto the Father, Which hath made us meet to be partakers of the inheritance of the saints in light:

Who hath <u>delivered us from</u> the power of darkness, and hath translated us into the kingdom of His dear Son:

Colossians 1:12, 13

Psychiatric Ward Avoided

"I am the father of four children: two boys aged 19 & 11 and two girls aged 16 & 10. I started a home-based contracting business to meet the needs of my family when the twenty years of working in the printing trade ended with layoffs. My first two contracts looked good, but both ended up being cancelled. I finally landed one job, but then there was nothing. My concern grew. I started to battle depression and lack of sleep. Sickness came in the form of a bladder infection and flu-like symptoms.

"Then I began losing my mind. It literally felt as if a physical part of the right side of my brain were missing and void. I started having difficulty with my cognitive abilities, and I noticed that ordinary mental activities were becoming increasingly difficult. I could not tie my shoes nor dial my cell phone to save my life. It was impossible for me to drive my car. Even walking became very challenging, and I had to have assistance. Then I lost my ability to communicate. I could not speak more than a few words before everything would come out as gibberish.

"I went to the emergency room of a local hospital. I had no idea what was wrong with me. They administered a number of tests, including a spinal tap and a CAT scan of my brain. Meanwhile, my wife was running down the list of contacts in my cell phone searching for people she could find to pray for us. She came across some pastors that we knew, and Nancy Insley came to mind.

"Meanwhile, in the emergency room with my eldest son at my side, the hospital continued to administer tests. Fear

gripped me, and I became violent as the psychiatrist talked of having me admitted to the psychiatric ward. My son read Scriptures to me to strengthen my heart. I knew the moment my friend Nancy entered the emergency area, as I could sense in my spirit that she was there. As she prayed for me, Nancy heard in her spirit that all this mess was being caused by a spirit of fear. When she asked if I was in fear about anything, I told her that I was terribly afraid of not being able to provide for the family and the possibility of losing our home.

"With authority, we came against the fear that had such a fierce grip on me. I was not allowed to speak any more words of fear, but only what God's Word said about me. For hours, I would not allow Nancy to stop praying, quoting Scripture and speaking soothing words of hope to me. If she paused to take a deep breath, I would grab her arm and command her to keep going, saying things like, 'Don't stop! You're helping me! You are pulling me through this!'

"After a few hours, the social worker assigned to me came into the room. When he did, I did something that no one expected: I rose up off of the bed in anger, tore the I.V. needle out of my arm and started to get dressed. I stated that I was going to leave—there was no way that they were going to lock me up! I got violent! Security was called, and they locked the double doors of the room that I was in. Then the peace of God came over me, and I calmed down enough to speak peaceably with the doctor.

"With continued encouragement from the Word being spoken to me, I was finally 'normal' enough to be released from the emergency room. With considerable reservations, the doctors sent me home. I was given prescriptions for sleep and for psychotic behavior. I chose only to take the medication for sleep, since I had not slept for so long.

"Upon arriving home, I went to bed and slept for a short time while Nancy and my wife sat in the living room,

talking and praying. As I slept, the spirit of fear came on me again, speaking lies to me. It said that everyone had abandoned me and that I had been asleep for days. Fears of all kinds were passing through my mind. In tears, I awoke and went downstairs only to find my wife and Nancy still praying.

"I was fed more Scripture and encouragement. We worked on getting my confession to line up with the Word of God. The Word of God became my Bread, and it was as if I were reading it for the very first time. It was alive to me! For the next two weeks, I had to combat fear with the Word. I would play music through the night that sang of the resurrection of Jesus and His Life conquering death and the grave!

"For those two weeks, when I would wake up in the middle of the night, the lies of fear would return. I started writing the lies down on paper; then I would find the Truth in the Word and confess it in order to combat the lie. With the Truth, I was able to keep my victory over fear. My strength has been renewed, and I am full of joy. My wife and I are feeding on God's Word like never before.

"Today, a year and a half later, I am still free from that spirit of fear. I have had opportunities to worry, but I no longer give place to it. My God shall supply all of my need according to His riches in glory through Christ Jesus, my Lord! (see Philippians 4:19). Fear is a weapon that the enemy uses, yet 'no weapon formed against me shall prosper, and every tongue which rises against me in judgment I shall condemn. This is my heritage and Jesus is my Lord. My righteousness is from Him.' says my Lord (see Isaiah 54:17)."—Robert

Who gave Himself for our sins, that He might <u>deliver</u> us from this present evil world, according to the will of God and our Father.

Galatians 1:4

And I heard a loud voice saying in heaven, "Now is come <u>salvation</u> *{health, deliverance, rescue, safety}*, and strength, and the kingdom of our God, and the power of His Christ: for the accuser of our brethren is cast down, which accused them before our God day and night. And they <u>overcame him by the blood of the Lamb</u>, and by the word of their testimony..."

Revelations 12:10, 11

But the salvation of the righteous is of the LORD: He is their Strength in the time of trouble. And the LORD shall help them, and deliver them: He shall deliver them from the wicked, and save them, because they trust in Him.

Psalm 37:39, 40

For [the Spirit which] you have now received [is] not a spirit of slavery to put you once more in bondage to fear, but you have received the Spirit of adoption [the Spirit producing sonship] in [the bliss of] which we cry, "Abba (Father)! Father!" *{Through Christ, we have been set free from all bondage.}*

Romans 8:15 AMP

We know [absolutely] that anyone born of God does not [deliberately and knowingly] practice committing sin, but the One Who was begotten of God carefully watches over *and* protects him..., and **the wicked one does not lay hold (get a grip) on him *or* touch [him]**. We know [positively] that we are of God, and the whole world [around us] is under the power of the evil one.

1 John 5:18, 19 AMP

Many evils confront the [consistently] righteous, but the Lord delivers him out of them **all**.

Psalm 34:19 AMP

In Him was Life; and the Life was the Light of men. *{"Life" here is "zoe", the God-kind of life. We are given that Life in Christ Jesus.}*

John 1:4

Always bearing about in the body the dying of the Lord Jesus, that the life also of Jesus might be made manifest in our body. For we which live are alway delivered unto death for Jesus' sake, that the life also of Jesus might be made manifest in our mortal flesh *{Both references to "life" here are that same "zoe" Life of God. Note that it is to be made manifest in our bodies.}*

2 Corinthians 4:10, 11

The LORD is my Shepherd; I shall not want.

Psalm 23:1

This poor man cried, and the LORD heard him, and saved him out of **all** his troubles. The angel of the LORD encampeth round about them that fear Him, and delivereth them. O taste and see that the LORD is good: blessed is the man that trusteth in Him. O fear the LORD, ye His saints: for there is **no want** to them that fear Him. The young lions do lack, and suffer hunger: but they that seek the LORD shall not want any good thing. *{Our health is a good thing!}*

Psalm 34:6-10

When Jesus therefore had received the vinegar, He said, "It is finished." *{Remittance of sin and freedom from curses (including sickness) were all finished!}*

John 19:30

"Let them shout for joy, and be glad, that favour My righteous cause: yea, let them say continually, 'Let the LORD be magnified, Which hath pleasure in the prosperity of His servant.'" *{"Prosperity" is the word "shalom", which means "safe, well, happy, welfare, i.e.* **health,** *prosperity, peace, favour, great,* **(good) health,** *prosper(-ity, -ous)", and more according to Strong's Concordance, word 07965.}*

Psalm 35:27

Blindness, Cataracts, Eye Ailments

I have seen countless numbers of people healed of blindness and other eye ailments, including the falling off of cataracts. One man was scheduled for surgery the morning after he was prayed for, but he was able to cancel the appointment because the cataracts had dropped off!

One very old woman in the Philippines was led forward for prayer. When I asked what she would like to be healed of, she said that she was blind. I laid hands on her eyes then instructed her to look out the window. She excitedly exclaimed that she could see way out into the field. She looked at me, leaned her head forward, pointing to it and said, "Do it again!" I did and then asked her to look out the window again. She said, "Now I can see way beyond the field!" *When she had entered the service, she was unable to see anything! She was so excited to get all that God had for her that she bent her head forward a third time for prayer. She was experiencing what is available to us through salvation!*

...If God *be* for us, who *can be* against us? *{What hold can the devil have on us if God is on our side?}*

Romans 8:31

He that dwelleth in the secret place of the most High shall abide under the shadow of the Almighty. I will say of the LORD, "He is my refuge and my fortress: my God; in Him will I trust." Surely He shall deliver thee from the snare of the fowler, and from the noisome pestilence. He shall cover thee with His feathers, and under His wings shalt thou trust: His truth shall be thy shield and buckler. Thou shalt not be afraid for the terror by night; nor for the arrow that flieth by day; nor for the pestilence that walketh in darkness; nor for the destruction that wasteth at noonday. A thousand shall fall at thy side, and ten thousand at thy right hand; but it shall not come nigh thee. Only with thine eyes shalt thou behold and see the reward of the wicked.
Because thou hast made the LORD, Which is my refuge, even the most High, thy habitation; there shall no evil befall thee, neither shall any plague come nigh thy dwelling. For He shall give His angels charge over thee, to keep thee in all thy ways. They shall bear thee up in their hands, lest thou dash thy foot against a stone. Thou shalt tread upon the lion and adder: the young lion and the dragon shalt thou trample under feet.
"Because he hath set his love upon Me, therefore will I deliver him: I will set him on high, because he hath known My Name. He shall call upon Me, and I will answer him: I will be with him in trouble; I will deliver him, and honour him. With long life will I satisfy him, and shew him My salvation."

Psalm 91:1-16

He Who did not withhold *or* spare [even] His own Son but gave Him up for us all, will He not also with Him freely *and* graciously give us **all** [other] things?

Romans 8:32 AMP

Yet amid all these things we are <u>more than conquerors</u> *and* gain a surpassing victory through Him Who loved us.

Romans 8:37 AMP

It is good that a man should both hope *{be expectant}* and quietly wait for the salvation of the LORD. *{"Salvation" means "victory, rescue, deliverance, help, salvation and safety". We can <u>expect</u> the victory of health.}*

Lamentations 3:26

Injured Ankle or the Promise of God?

"I was working in the garden when I stepped onto the edge of the pavement with my foot lengthwise. My ankle snapped, and I fell to the ground with all of my tools flying out of my hands. The ankle immediately swelled up, and it was very painful. Knowing what God's Word says, I immediately came against the pain and the injury. I let the devil know that I was not accepting broken bones but that I was walking in health.

"In great pain, I scooted up the driveway into the house. I got onto the bed with my foot propped up and spoke with the Lord. I told Him that I trusted Him and that I had seen Him heal many bones instantly. I trusted His Word that my ankle, too, was healed. The Lord spoke to me saying, 'When you pray for others, you expect them to act on their faith. Get up and walk.' Well, that is exactly what I did! The ankle showed the physical signs of the injury, as far as swelling and the pooling of blood, for several days; but the foot was perfectly healed. The next morning, I was out gardening again! In all of this, I never considered going to a doctor for X-rays and a cast. Why should I? I am in covenant with the Lord!"—Nancy Insley

..."Thy **faith** hath saved thee; go in peace." *{"Saved" here is again "sozo", meaning healed or to be made whole, delivered, protected and preserved.}*

Luke 7:50

Now we have received, not the spirit of the world, but the Spirit which is of God; that we might know the things that are freely given to us of God *{like healing}*. Which things also we speak, not in the words which man's wisdom teacheth, but which the Holy Ghost teacheth; comparing spiritual things with spiritual. *{Healing is spiritual. It is part of our free gift of salvation.}*

1 Corinthians 2:12, 13

Know ye not that your bodies are the members of Christ? ...What? know ye not that your body is the temple of the Holy Ghost which is in you, which ye have of God, and ye are not your own? For ye are bought with a price: therefore glorify God in your body, and in your spirit, which are God's. *{God is not glorified by a deformed or sickly body.}*

1 Corinthians 6:15a, 19, 20

Know ye not that ye are the temple of God, and that the Spirit of God dwelleth in you?

1 Corinthians 3:16

In whom the god of this world hath blinded the minds of them which believe not, lest the light of the glorious Gospel of Christ, Who is the image of God, should shine unto them. *{Satan loves to deceive us into believing that God does not always want to heal us. Satan's world is full of sin, lies, sickness and trouble. Why is it that there is no sin, lying, sickness, nor trouble in heaven? There God reigns.}*

2 Corinthians 4:4

But now hath He obtained a more excellent ministry, by how much also He is the Mediator of a <u>better covenant</u>, which was established upon <u>better promises</u>. *{Under the Old Covenant, the Jews were offered healing; how much more are we promised under the New Covenant!}*

Hebrews 8:6

"I assure you, most solemnly I tell you, if anyone steadfastly believes in Me, he will himself be able to do the things that I do; and he will do **even greater** things than these, because I go to the Father." *{And consider what Jesus was doing: teaching, preaching, healing, performing miracles and raising people from the dead!}*

John 14:12 AMP

THE WILL OF GOD

God's Will Pertaining to Healing

...with Whom is no variableness, neither shadow of turning.

And God said, "Let Us make man in Our image, after Our likeness..." So God created man in His own image, in the image of God created He him... And God saw every thing that He had made, and, behold, it was very good. *{That is, without defect, deformity, sickness or weakness.}*

Genesis 1:26, 27, 31a

(Eve responding to the serpent:) "But of the fruit of the tree which is in the midst of the garden, God hath said, 'Ye shall not eat of it, neither shall ye touch it, lest ye die.'" *{Death, sin and sickness all entered the earth the moment man ate of the forbidden tree.}*

Genesis 3:3

(Jesus is) the Word of <u>Life</u>. *{He brings <u>us</u> life and that more abundantly.}*

1 John 1:1

For the law of the Spirit of Life in Christ Jesus hath made me free from the law of sin and death. *{The Spirit of Life brings us health—not sickness, disease, pain nor death.}*

Romans 8:2

...that He might make thee know that man doth not live by bread only, but by every <u>Word</u> that proceedeth out of the mouth of the LORD doth man **live**.

Deuteronomy 8:3

For with You is the fountain of <u>life</u>;

Psalm 36:9a AMP

For once you were darkness, but now you are light in the Lord; walk as children of Light...

Ephesians 5:8 AMP

There is therefore now no condemnation to them which are in Christ Jesus, <u>who walk not after the flesh</u>, but after the Spirit. *{The Spirit agrees with the will of God.}*

Romans 8:1

Pain Kept Her Awake Each Night

An elderly lady in Germany came up for prayer, because she suffered such great pain every night that she hardly slept. The next morning, she came to the service glowing and excited: She had slept the entire night with no pain, and she woke up with tremendous joy!

Now we have received, not the spirit of the world, but the Spirit which is of God; that we might know the things that are freely given to us of God *{like healing}*. Which things

26

also we speak, not in the words which man's wisdom teacheth, but which the Holy Ghost teacheth; comparing spiritual things with spiritual. *{Healing is spiritual. God says in Zechariah 4:6 that it is "not by might, nor by power, but by My Spirit." By following His Spirit, we can carry on the same works of healing which Jesus did.}*

1 Corinthians 2:12, 13

Behold, what manner of <u>love</u> the Father hath bestowed upon us, that we should be called the sons of God... *{Love would not make sick, but love would heal. The children of God should be more prosperous and healthy than those without this loving God.}*

1 John 3:1

But God—so rich is He in His mercy! Because of *and* in order to satisfy the great *and* wonderful *and* intense love with which He loved us, *{We do not make <u>our</u> children sick out of our great love for them!}*

Ephesians 2:4 AMP

We know [absolutely] that anyone born of God does not [deliberately and knowingly] practice committing sin, but the One Who was begotten of God carefully watches over *and* protects him..., and **the wicked one does not lay hold (get a grip) on him *or* touch [him]**. We know [positively] that we are of God, and the whole world [around us] is under the power of the evil one.

1 John 5:18, 19 AMP

For this <u>purpose</u> the Son of God was manifested, that He might **destroy** the works of the devil. *{The works of the devil are sickness, fear, death, frustration, lies, pain, disease, depression, and more. They have been destroyed that we might live free of them.}*

1 John 3:8b

27

"Thy kingdom come. <u>Thy will be done in earth,</u> as it is in heaven."

Matthew 6:10

Jesus saith unto them, "My meat is to do the will of Him that sent Me, and to finish His work." *{Jesus only healed.}*

John 4:34

So Jesus answered them by saying, "I assure you, most solemnly I tell you, the Son is <u>able</u> to do nothing of Himself (of His own accord); but He is <u>able</u> to do only what He sees the Father doing, for whatever the Father does is what the Son does in the same way [in His turn.]." *{Jesus was only able to heal and not to make sick.}*

John 5:19 AMP

"I can of Mine own self do nothing...I seek not Mine own will, but the will of the Father which hath sent Me." *{Jesus only healed.}*

John 5:30

"For I came down from heaven, not to do Mine own will, but the will of Him that sent Me." *{God's will was to heal.}*

John 6:38

Jesus answered them by saying, "My teaching is not My own, but His Who sent Me." *{Although people say that God was teaching them through an illness, Jesus never taught by making His disciples nor the multitudes sick first. We learn far better when we feel good.}*

John 7:16 AMP

So Jesus added, "When you have lifted up the Son of Man [on the cross], you will realize (know, understand) that I am He [for Whom you look] and that <u>I do nothing of Myself</u> (of My own accord or on My own authority), but I say [exactly] what My Father has taught Me. And He Who sent Me is ever with Me; My Father has not left Me alone, for <u>I always do what pleases Him</u>." *{Jesus did nothing on His own; He only did the will of His Father. Jesus healed and <u>only</u> healed; He did not make ill. It was the will of the Father to heal all.}*

John 8:28, 29 AMP

"I speak that which I have seen with my Father..." *{He only commanded healing, never sickness.}*

John 8:38

"This is because I have never spoken on My own authority *or* of My own accord *or* as self-appointed, but the Father Who sent Me has Himself given Me orders [concerning] what to say and what to tell. And I know that His commandment is (means) eternal life. So whatever I speak, I am saying [exactly] what My Father has told Me to say *and* in accordance with His instructions." *{He never instructed us that healing was not for everyone. He healed them all.}*

John 12:49, 50 AMP

Issue of Blood

"I have been healed before. I saw my broken foot with bones sticking out be totally restored in four hours. I was in great pain. With tears streaming down my face, all I could say over and over was, 'By His stripes, I am healed, in Jesus' Name.' My foot was black and  *blue, but I had absolutely no pain. I even taught a seminar the next day.*

"Having experienced this, I knew God's Word was true. I applied the same faith to hemorrhaging I was challenged

with, but I was falling short of seeing it stop. I went to Nancy's healing class. Nancy prayed for me, and she told me that all of God's promises are mine; I only needed to <u>believe</u> they were mine. I started confessing what God said instead of what the doctors had said. The next day, I could already notice a difference. I kept confessing His Word: 'Lord, I believe that Your promises are mine. I walk in total heath, nothing missing and nothing broken. I will live long and strong, in Jesus' Name.' It took a week, but the bleeding completely stopped. May we all stand on the promises He has given us and walk in total health."— Jody

Two other women in the last few years have also suffered from uncontrollable bleeding. Both were healed instantly and reported the victory the following day.

"Do you not believe that I am in the Father, and that the Father is in Me? What I am telling you I do not say on My own authority *and* of My own accord; but the Father Who lives continually in Me does the (*His*) works (His own miracles, deeds of power)." *{Jesus only ever did the will of the Father. He never made anyone ill, diseased nor hurt.}*

John 14:10 AMP

...He generously bestows His riches upon **all** who call upon Him [in faith].

Romans 10:12 AMP

And, behold, there came a leper and worshiped Him, saying, "Lord, if Thou wilt, Thou canst make me clean." And Jesus put forth His hand, and touched him, saying, "I will; be thou clean." And immediately his leprosy was cleansed.

Matthew 8:2, 3

And it came to pass, when He was in a certain city, behold a man full of leprosy: who seeing Jesus fell on his face, and besought Him, saying, "Lord, if Thou wilt, Thou canst make me clean." And He put forth His hand, and touched him, saying, "I will: be thou clean." And immediately the leprosy departed from him. *{The leper clearly had faith.}*

Luke 5:12, 13

And a leper came to Him, begging Him on his knees and saying to Him, "If You are willing, You are able to make me clean." And being moved with pity *and* sympathy, Jesus reached out His hand and touched him, and said to him, "I am willing; be made clean!" And at once the leprosy [completely] left him and he was made clean [by being healed]. *{The leper had faith in the Word of Jesus.}*

Mark 1:40-42 AMP

People Leaving Their Wheelchairs

I have seen a number of people get out of wheelchairs and walk. One man got up out of his wheelchair and came walking into the church the following night for the next meeting. This is God's will!

"For the Son of man is not come to destroy men's lives, but to save them." *{God's will is to save (sozo) us and to bring us healing.}*

Luke 9:56a

For He does not willingly *and* from His heart afflict or grieve the children of men.

Lamentations 3:33

And the LORD will take away from thee **all** sickness, and will put none of the evil diseases of Egypt, which thou knowest, upon thee...

Deuteronomy 7:15

He sent His Word, and healed them, and delivered them from their destructions. *{Jesus is the Word which was sent; He has already healed us.}*

Psalm 107:20

[God] disarmed the principalities and powers that were ranged against us and made a bold display and public example of them, in triumphing over them in Him and in it [the cross].

Colossians 2:15 AMP

Christ hath redeemed us from the curse of the law... *{Sickness and disease were part of the curse. God wants to give us Life; Satan only wants to steal it away.}*

Galatians 3:13

"I do not ask that You will take them out of the world, but that You will keep and <u>protect them from the evil one</u>. They are not of the world (worldly, belonging to the world), [just] as I am not of the world. Sanctify them [purify, consecrate, separate them for Yourself, make them holy] by Truth; Your Word is Truth." *{Through His death, Jesus conquered Satan, and we are more than conquerors through Him (Romans 8:37). We have already won the battle!}*

John 17:15-17 AMP

Beloved, I pray that you may prosper in **every** way and [that your body] may keep well, even as [I know] your soul keeps well *and* prospers.

3 John 1:2 AMP

Beloved, I wish above all things that thou mayest prosper and be in health, even as thy soul prospereth.

3 John 1:2

"And now come I to thee; and <u>these things I speak</u> in the world, that they might have My joy fulfilled in themselves."

John 17:13

"In the world ye shall have tribulation: but be of good cheer; I have overcome the world."

John 16:33

But as it is written, "Eye hath not seen, nor ear heard, neither have entered into the heart of man, the things which God hath prepared for them that love Him." *{One of those things He has prepared for us is healing.}*

1 Corinthians 2:9

And be not conformed to this world: but be ye transformed by the renewing of your mind, that ye may prove what is that good, and acceptable, and perfect, will of God. *{Let your mind be renewed now. Do not conform to the erroneous thoughts of this world.}*

Romans 12:2

But we have the mind of Christ (the Messiah) *and* do hold the thoughts (feelings and purposes) of His heart. *{The purpose of His heart was to provide us with health. Having the mind of Christ, we can accept this.}*

1 Corinthians 2:16b AMP

Then Peter opened his mouth, and said, "Of a truth I perceive that God is no respecter of persons." *{He wants to heal all.}*

Acts 10:34

For God shows no partiality... *{If God did not deny healing to those in Jesus' day, He will not deny healing to us today.}*

Romans 2:11 AMP

...there is no respect of persons (no partiality) with Him.

Ephesians 6:9b AMP

"My Ankle Snapped"

"A few months ago, I was visiting a friend when I stepped poorly off a step. My ankle snapped, and I lay helpless outside the house in pain. My friend called my mom (Nancy), who had to drive over to where I was. Together we believed for healing and prayed. Immediately the pain stopped, and I was able to hobble into the house. Within an hour, the ankle felt so good that I left the house and drove out into the country. A couple of hours later, I was able to put on dress shoes and to go to the evening church service!

"Over the last few years, I have experienced repeated healings of migraines, flu symptoms, aches, pains, fears, menstrual cramps, a fractured foot arch and joint pain. God is so faithful!"—Christa

Jesus Christ the same yesterday, and to day, and for ever. *{He will <u>continue</u> to heal us, protect us, etc.}*

Hebrews 13:8

"For I am the Lord, I do not change..." *{He is still Love, still wanting our best, and still wanting us healed.}*

Malachi 3:6 AMP

There hath no temptation taken you but such as is common to man: but God is faithful, Who will not suffer you to be tempted above that ye are able; but will with the temptation also make a way to escape, that ye may be able to bear it. *{"Temptation" here is "a putting to proof" or "adversity". There is no indication that it is referring to sickness. Even if it were, God would make a way of escape (through our authority over the evil one and through His promises).}*

1 Corinthians 10:13

Let no one say when he is tempted, "I am tempted from God;" for God is incapable of being tempted by [what is] evil and He Himself tempts no one. *{These last two verses show that God is not doing the tempting. If He would never tempt us, why would He plague us with sickness?}*

James 1:13 AMP

But thanks be to God, Who in Christ **always** leads us in triumph [as trophies of Christ's victory] and through us spreads *and* makes evident the fragrance of the knowledge of God everywhere. *{Divine health is a beautiful fragrance to carry.}*

2 Corinthians 2:14 AMP

Now the Lord is the Spirit, and where the Spirit of the Lord is, there is **liberty** (emancipation from bondage, freedom). [Isa. 61:1, 2] *{When we bind the spirit of infirmity, fear, etc. through the Name of the Lord and have His Spirit in us, we **will** be made free!}*

2 Corinthians 3:17 AMP

Stand fast therefore in the liberty wherewith Christ hath made us free, and be not entangled again with the yoke of bondage.

Galatians 5:1

And hath raised us up together, and made us sit together in heavenly places in Christ Jesus... *{We are seated with Christ. He does not want His Body filled with sickness and disease.}*

Ephesians 2:6

"But ye shall receive <u>power</u>, after that the Holy Ghost is come upon you..."

Acts 1:8

May He grant you out of the rich treasury of His glory to be strengthened *and* reinforced with <u>mighty power</u> in the <u>inner</u> man by the [Holy] Spirit [Himself indwelling your innermost being and personality]. *{His mighty power resides in us! Faith will activate it.}*

Ephesians 3:16 AMP

Now unto Him that is able to do exceeding abundantly above **all** that we ask or think, according to the <u>power</u> that worketh in <u>us</u>...

Ephesians 3:20

"And now, Lord, ...grant to Your bond servants [full freedom] to declare Your message fearlessly. While You stretch out <u>Your hand to cure and to perform signs and wonders</u> through the authority and by the **power** of the Name of Your Holy Child and servant Jesus."

Acts 4:29, 30 AMP

But the Lord is <u>faithful</u>, Who shall stablish you, and <u>keep you</u> from evil.

2 Thessalonians 3:3

...You have loosed my bonds.

Psalm 116:16b AMP

"With whom My hand shall be established *and* ever abide; My arm also shall strengthen him. The <u>enemy</u> shall not exact from him *or* do him violence *or* outwit him, nor shall the wicked afflict *and* humble him."

Psalm 89:21, 22 AMP

"My covenant will I not break, nor alter the thing that is gone out of My lips."

Psalm 89:34

...upholding all things by the word of His power... *{This means: bringing forth **all** things by the word of His miracle-working power. This includes healing.}*

Hebrews 1:3

And he said, "Blessed be the LORD God of Israel, Who hath with His hands fulfilled that which He spake with His mouth..."

2 Chronicles 6:4

"...for the mouth of the LORD has spoken it." *{What the Lord speaks is of great importance and is **true**. For example, "By the stripes of Jesus, you are healed!"}*

Isaiah 40:5

The LORD of hosts hath sworn, saying, "Surely as I have thought, so shall it come to pass; and as I have purposed, so shall it stand." *{He has purposed our healing, and so shall it stand.}*

Isaiah 14:24

"The grass withereth, the flower fadeth: but the Word of our God shall stand for ever."

Isaiah 40:8

It is because of the Lord's mercy *and* loving-kindness that we are not consumed, because His [tender] compassions fail not. They are new every morning; great *and* abundant is Your stability *and* faithfulness. "The Lord is my portion *or* share," says my living being (my inner self); "therefore will I hope in Him *and* wait expectantly for Him." The Lord is good to those who wait hopefully *and* expectantly for Him, to those who seek Him...

Lamentations 3:22-25 AMP

Asthma Healed

Many have come with asthma and other lung problems like bronchitis and lung cancer. They were instantly healed, being able to take deep breaths and to run around.

A child with asthma was filled with great joy when she could take big, deep breaths!

One woman in Croatia, suffering from extreme asthma, struggled with every breath that she took. After I laid hands on her, I had her take a deep breath. As she sucked her lungs full of air, her eyes got big. She sucked  *in again....and again....and again. She could not contain the joy of taking deep breaths of oxygen and was overcome with excitement. She didn't know what to do with herself. Then she threw up her arms, praising God with extreme joy radiating from her countenance and tears of thankfulness and joy running down her cheeks.*

...there hath not failed one Word of all His good promise...

1 Kings 8:56

"...I will visit you, and keep My good promise to you... For I know the thoughts *and* plans that I have for you," says the Lord, "thoughts *and* plans for welfare *and* peace *{lit.: health, welfare, wholeness, prosperity, peace, rest and safety}* and <u>not</u> for evil, to give you hope in your final outcome. Then you will call upon Me, and you will come and pray to Me, and I will hear *and* heed you. Then you will see Me, inquire for *and* require Me [as a vital necessity] and find Me when you search for Me with all your heart."

Jeremiah 29:10-13 AMP

"So shall My Word be that goeth forth out of My mouth: it shall not return unto Me void, but it shall accomplish that which I please, and it shall prosper in the thing whereto I sent it." *{Will not return "void" means will not return "without being effective". God's Word will not return to Him without being effective and accomplishing what He desired. What a wonderful promise!}*

Isaiah 55:11

...revive *and* stimulate me according to Your Word!

Psalm 119:25b AMP

The LORD upholdeth <u>all</u> that fall, and raiseth up <u>all</u> those that be bowed down.

Psalm 145:14

And shall say to them: "Hear, O Israel, you draw near this day to battle against your enemies. Let not your [minds and] hearts faint; fear not, and do not tremble or be terrified [and in dread] because of them. For the Lord your God is He Who goes with you to fight for you against your enemies to save you." *{Our enemies are the messengers of Satan.}*

Deuteronomy 20:3, 4 AMP

Then they cried to the Lord in their trouble, and He saved them out of their distresses. He brought them out of darkness and the shadow of death and <u>broke apart</u> the bonds that held them. *{This includes the bonds of sickness and disease.}*

Psalm 107:13, 14 AMP

And the Lord turned the <u>captivity</u> of Job <u>*and*</u> restored his fortunes, when he prayed for his friends; also the Lord gave Job twice as much as he had before. *{Both sickness and poverty were a part of his captivity to the devil.}*

Job 42:10 AMP

For You deliver an afflicted *and* humble people...

Psalm 18:27 AMP

If they obey and serve Him, they shall spend their days in prosperity, and their years in pleasures. *{Sickness is not a pleasure.}*

Job 36:11

Let the redeemed of the LORD say so, whom He hath redeemed from the hand of the enemy; *{That's us! The enemy cannot touch us, if we do not allow it.}*

Psalm 107:2

"**No** weapon that is formed against thee shall prosper..."

Isaiah 54:17

But He, knowing their thoughts, said unto them, "Every kingdom divided against itself is brought to desolation; and a house divided against a house falleth. If Satan also be divided against himself, how shall his kingdom stand?" *{If sickness were of God, Jesus would be dividing His Kingdom by healing the very ones God had made sick.}*

Luke 11:17, 18

"When the strong man, fully armed, ...guards his own dwelling, his belongings are undisturbed... But when one stronger than he attacks him and conquers him, he robs him of his whole armor on which he had relied and divides up *and* distributes all his goods as plunder (spoil)."

Luke 11:21, 22 AMP

...You Who deliver the poor *and* the afflicted from him who is too strong for him...from him who snatches away his goods? *{God delivers us from the strongman who afflicts us and snatches away our health.}*

Psalm 35:10 AMP

And it shall come to pass in that day, that his burden shall be taken away from off thy shoulder, and his yoke from off thy neck, and the yoke shall be <u>destroyed</u> because of the anointing.

Isaiah 10:27

For Thou hast <u>broken</u> the yoke of his burden,

Isaiah 9:4a

But He turned, and said unto Peter, "Get thee behind Me, Satan: thou art an offence unto Me: for thou savourest not the things that be of God, but those that be of men." *{Don't agree with what the devil is speaking to you!}*

Matthew 16:23

Thy mercy, O LORD, is in the heavens; and Thy faithfulness reacheth unto the clouds. *{He is faithful to perform His Word.}*

Psalm 36:5

No good thing will He withhold from those who walk uprightly.

Psalm 84:11b AMP

...let us hold fast our profession. For we have not an High Priest which cannot be touched with the feeling of our infirmities; but was in all points tempted like as we are, yet without sin. Let us therefore come boldly unto the throne of grace, that we may obtain mercy, and find grace to help in time of need. *{Jesus understands—He had the same temptations to be sick, but He did not sin; He resisted. He will answer our prayers for grace to resist.}*

Hebrews 4:14b-16

Arthritis Pain Leaves

Many have come with various kinds of arthritis, including rheumatoid arthritis, or rheumatism, and they were all healed. One evening, after prayer, I asked a little boy who had had arthritis in the knee to move it around. He looked frightened and shook his head, because he knew the pain it normally caused him. His friends, however, encouraged him to try moving it. As he started to flex his knee, he was amazed that there was no longer any pain!

One man had arthritis in the knee plus pain in his left hip as well as pain in his right leg. All pain left each area.

A lady with arthritis in the hand could only bend one finger. After prayer, I asked her to make a fist. When she couldn't, I asked the Lord what to do. I then told her to roll her arm back and forth. Immediately, her hand was healed with full mobility!

Another woman was in tears because she could not move her index finger. After prayer, she was able to flex it, completely healed.

God be merciful unto us, and bless us; and cause His face to shine upon us; Selah. *{Sickness is not a blessing, nor does it represent God's graciousness nor His mercy.}*

Psalm 67:1

That Thy way may be known upon earth, Thy saving
health among all nations. *{The word "health" here means:
health, welfare, aid, deliverance, victory and prosperity.
All of this is available to us!}*

Psalm 67:2

The blessing of the Lord—it makes [truly] rich, and He
adds **no** sorrow with it... *{Our health is a blessing; He
adds no sorrow to it. According to Strong's, word 6087,
"sorrow" means: an earthen vessel; usually (painful) toil;
also a pang (whether of body or mind): grievous, idol,
labor, sorrow.}*

Proverbs 10:22 AMP

According as His divine power hath <u>given unto us **all**
things that pertain unto **life** and godliness,</u> through the
knowledge of Him that hath called us to glory and virtue:
Whereby are <u>given unto us exceeding great and precious
promises: that by these ye might be partakers of the divine
nature, having escaped the corruption that is in the world</u>
through lust. *{Most of the promises have been given to us
for this life <u>right now</u> when we need them.}* And beside
this, giving all diligence, add to your faith virtue; and to
virtue knowledge; and to knowledge temperance; and to
temperance patience; and to patience godliness; and to
godliness brotherly kindness; and to brotherly kindness
charity. For if these things be in you, and <u>abound</u>, they
make you that ye shall neither be barren nor unfruitful in
the knowledge of our Lord Jesus Christ. But he that
lacketh these things is blind, and cannot see afar off, and
hath forgotten that he was purged from his old sins.
Wherefore the rather, brethren, give diligence to make
your calling and election sure: for <u>if ye do these things, ye
shall never fall</u>:

2 Peter 1:3-10

God is not a man, that He should lie; neither the son of man, that He should repent: hath He said, and shall He not do it? or hath He spoken, and shall He not make it good?

Numbers 23:19

For all the promises of God in Him are "yea," and in Him "Amen," unto the glory of God by us.

2 Corinthians 1:20

Do not, therefore, fling away your fearless confidence, for it carries a great *and* glorious compensation of reward. For you have need of steadfast patience *and* endurance, so that you may perform *and* **fully** accomplish the **will** of God, and thus receive *and* carry away [and enjoy to the full] what is promised. *{It is God's will for you to walk in health.}*

Hebrews 10:35, 36 AMP

<u>Do not err</u>, my beloved brethren. Every good gift and every perfect gift is from above, and cometh down from the Father of lights, with Whom is no variableness, neither shadow of turning. *{This follows the verses that state that God does not tempt us with evil. Sickness is evil. It is not a good gift; it is **not** from God! Jesus said, "...he that hath seen Me hath seen the Father," and He **never** placed a sickness onto anyone. Jesus never "reversed" a work of God, only the works of the devil.}*

James 1:16, 17

And the very God of peace sanctify you wholly; and I pray God your whole <u>spirit</u> and <u>soul</u> and **<u>body</u>** be preserved blameless unto the coming of our Lord Jesus Christ. <u>Faithful</u> is He that calleth you, Who also will do it. *{"Blameless" means "faultlessly", according to Strong's Concordance, word 274.}*

1 Thessalonians 5:23, 24

HEALING

Scripture Verses Showing God's Healing

"For I am the Lord, I change not."

"...I am the LORD that healeth thee."

Exodus 15:26

The law of the Lord is perfect, restoring the [whole] person... *{That is, body, soul and spirit.}*

Psalm 19:7 AMP

He keepeth **all** his bones: not one of them is broken.

Psalm 34:20

Surely He shall <u>deliver</u> thee from the snare of the fowler, and from the noisome pestilence.

Psalm 91:3

Because thou hast made the LORD, Which is my refuge, even the most High, thy habitation; there shall <u>no evil</u>

befall thee, <u>neither shall any plague</u> come nigh thy dwelling.

Psalm 91:9, 10

"With **long life** will I satisfy him and shew him my salvation."

Psalm 91:16

Bless the LORD, O my soul, and forget not all His benefits: Who forgiveth **all** thine iniquities; Who healeth **all** thy diseases;

Psalm 103:2, 3

"But unto you that fear My Name shall the Sun of righteousness arise with healing in His wings..."

Malachi 4:2

And it came to pass after these things, that the son of the woman, the mistress of the house, fell sick; and his sickness was so sore, that there was no breath left in him. And he [Elijah] said unto her, "Give me thy son." And he took him out of her bosom, and carried him up into a loft, where he abode, and laid him upon his own bed. And he stretched himself upon the child three times, and cried unto the LORD, and said, "O LORD my God, I pray thee, let this child's soul come into him again." And the LORD heard the voice of Elijah; and the soul of the child came into him again, and he revived. And Elijah took the child, and brought him down out of the chamber into the house, and delivered him unto his mother: and Elijah said, "See, thy son liveth."

1 Kings 17:17, 19, 21-23

And he said, "What then is to be done for her?" And Gehazi answered, "Verily she hath no child, and her husband is old." And he said, "Call her." And when he had called her, she stood in the door. And he said, "About this season, according to the time of life, thou shalt embrace a son." And she said, "Nay, my lord, thou man of God, do not lie unto thine handmaid." And the woman conceived, and bare a son at that season that Elisha had said unto her, according to the time of life.

2 Kings 4:14-17

Dizziness, "Brain Fog", Fatigue and Infertility

"In June of 2006, Nancy taught my family about healing. I had had a long list of strange symptoms, and I did not know the cause. My sister and her husband, who also attended the meeting, had tried unsuccessfully for four years to conceive a child.

"After receiving prayer that night, I began to improve as symptoms gradually started disappearing: I was no longer dizzy, the 'brain fog' lifted, fatigue was gone, and symptoms of PMS eased. Another problem I had had was suffering allergies when mowing the lawn. Applying the teaching, I began to take authority over my body saying, 'In the Name of Jesus, the air I breathe while mowing will not have any ill effect on me. I do not receive any allergies. By Jesus' stripes I was healed. Thank you, Lord, and bless my work.' Since then, I do not even sneeze during or after mowing!

"Also, my sister got pregnant three months after that prayer. Their baby was born strong and healthy at 10 pounds 3 ounces. Now I babysit my little miracle nephew. Such a blessing! And I have gotten stronger as a result of carrying him around!"—Olga

And when he had taken him, and brought him to his mother, he sat on her knees till noon, and then died. And when Elisha was come into the house, behold, the child was dead, and laid upon his bed. He went in therefore, and shut the door upon them twain, and prayed unto the LORD. And he went up, and lay upon the child, and put his mouth upon his mouth, and his eyes upon his eyes, and his hands upon his hands: and he stretched himself upon the child; and the flesh of the child waxed warm. Then he returned, and walked in the house to and fro; and went up, and stretched himself upon him: and the child sneezed seven times, and the child opened his eyes.

2 Kings 4:20, 32-35

(Referring to God bringing His people out of Egypt:) He brought them forth also with silver and gold, and there was **not one feeble** person among their tribes.

Psalm 105:37

And one of them smote the servant of the high priest, and cut off his right ear. And Jesus answered and said, "Suffer ye thus far." And He touched his ear, and healed him.

Luke 22:50, 51

And when Jesus was come into Peter's house, He saw his wife's mother laid, and sick of a fever. And He touched her hand, and the fever left her; and she arose, and ministered unto them.

Matthew 8:14, 15

(Simon's mother-in-law:) And He came and took her by the hand, and lifted her up; and immediately the fever left her, and she ministered unto them.

Mark 1:31

And He arose out of the synagogue, and entered Simon's house. And Simon's wife's mother was taken with a great fever; and they besought Him for her. And He stood over her, and rebuked the fever; and it left her: and immediately she arose and ministered unto them.

Luke 4:38, 39

"Take My yoke...for I am meek and lowly in heart: and ye shall find rest unto your souls. For My yoke is easy and My burden is light." *{Giving us sicknesses would not be making our burdens light.}*

Matthew 11:29, 30

But the angel said unto him, "Fear not, Zacharias: for thy prayer is heard; and thy wife Elisabeth shall bear thee a son, and thou shalt call his name John." And after those days his wife Elisabeth conceived, and hid herself five months...

Luke 1:13, 24

Then was brought unto Him one possessed with a <u>devil</u>, blind, and dumb: and He healed him, insomuch that the blind and dumb both spake and saw.

Matthew 12:22

Insomuch that the multitude wondered, when they saw the dumb to speak, the maimed to be whole, the lame to walk, and the blind to see: and they glorified the God of Israel.

Matthew 15:31

And Jesus stopped and called them, and asked, "What do you want Me to do for you?" They answered Him, "Lord, we want our eyes to be opened!" And Jesus, in pity, touched their eyes; and instantly they received their sight and followed Him.

Matthew 20:32-34 AMP

And it came to pass, that as He was come nigh unto Jericho, a certain blind man sat by the way side begging: And hearing the multitude pass by, he asked what it meant. And they told him, that Jesus of Nazareth passeth by. And he cried, saying, "Jesus, thou Son of David, have mercy on me." And they which went before rebuked him, that he should hold his peace: but he cried so much the more, "Thou Son of David, have mercy on me."

And Jesus stood, and commanded him to be brought unto Him: and when he was come near, He asked him, Saying, "What wilt thou that I shall do unto thee?" And he said, "Lord, that I may receive my sight." And Jesus said unto him, "Receive thy sight: thy faith hath saved thee." And immediately he received his sight, and followed Him, glorifying God: and all the people, when they saw it, gave praise unto God.

Luke 18:35-43

"She Could Not Open Her Mouth"

"One woman's mouth and teeth were so bad that she could not open her mouth. As soon as she was prayed for, all that was loosed, and she could freely open her mouth."—Angelika

And they came to Jericho: and as He went out of Jericho with His disciples and a great number of people, blind Bartimaeus, the son of Timaeus, sat by the highway side begging. And when he heard that it was Jesus of Nazareth, he began to cry out, and say, "Jesus, thou Son of David, have mercy on me." And many charged him that he should hold his peace: but he cried the more a great deal, "Thou Son of David, have mercy on me."

And Jesus stood still, and commanded him to be called. And they call the blind man, saying unto him, "Be of good comfort, rise; He calleth thee." And he, casting away his garment, rose, and came to Jesus. And Jesus answered and said unto him, "What wilt thou that I should do unto thee?" The blind man said unto him, "Lord, that I might receive my sight." And Jesus said unto him, "Go thy way; thy faith hath made thee whole." And immediately he received his sight, and followed Jesus in the way.

Mark 10:46-52

And He went forward and touched the funeral bier, and the pallbearers stood still. And He said, "Young man, I say to you, 'Arise [from death]!'"

Luke 7:14 AMP

And when He thus had spoken, He cried with a loud voice, "Lazarus, come forth." And he that was dead came forth, bound hand and foot with graveclothes: and his face was bound about with a napkin. Jesus saith unto them, "Loose him, and let him go."

John 11:43, 44

(Nobleman:) When he heard that Jesus was come out of Judaea into Galilee, he went unto Him, and besought Him that He would come down, and heal his son: for he was at the point of death. The nobleman saith unto Him, "Sir, come down ere my child die." Jesus saith unto him, "Go thy way; thy son liveth." And the man believed the word that Jesus had spoken unto him, and he went his way.

John 4:47, 49, 50

(Lame man at pool:) Jesus said to him, "Get up! Pick up your bed (sleeping pad) and walk!" *[The man responded in faith by getting up.]*

John 5:8 AMP

And He healed many that were sick of divers diseases, and cast out many devils...

Mark 1:34

And in that same hour He cured many of their infirmities and plagues, and of evil spirits; and unto many that were blind He gave sight. Then Jesus answering said unto them, "Go your way, and tell John what things ye have seen and heard; how that the blind see, the lame walk, the lepers are cleansed, the deaf hear, the dead are raised, to the poor the Gospel is preached."

Luke 7:21, 22

But the centurion replied to Him, "Lord, I am not worthy *or* fit to have You come under my roof; but only speak the word, and my servant boy will be cured." "...I have not found so much **faith** as this with anyone, even in Israel." Then to the centurion Jesus said, "Go; it shall be done for you as you have believed." And the servant boy was restored to health at that very moment.

Matthew 8:8, 10, 13 AMP

"But [just] speak a word, and my servant boy **will be healed**"... Now when Jesus heard this, He marveled at him, and He turned and said to the crowd that followed Him, "I tell you, not even in [all] Israel have I found such great **faith** [as this]." And when the messengers...returned to the house, they found the bond servant *who had been ill* quite well again.

Luke 7:7b, 9, 10 AMP

And, behold, there was a man which had his hand withered. And they asked Him, saying, "Is it lawful to heal on the sabbath days?" that they might accuse Him. Then saith He to the man, "Stretch forth thine hand." And he stretched it forth; and it was restored whole, like as the other. *{This man acted on his faith.}*

Matthew 12:10, 13

...and He said to the man with the withered hand, "Come and stand here in the midst." And he arose and stood there. ...[Jesus] said to the man, "Stretch out your hand!" And he did so, and his hand was fully restored *like the other one.*

Luke 6:8, 10 AMP

...and [Jesus] said to the man, "Hold out your hand." He held it out, and his hand was [completely] restored.

Mark 3:5 AMP

And when Jesus came into the ruler's house, and saw the minstrels and the people making a noise, He said unto them, "Give place: for the maid is not dead, but sleepeth." And they laughed Him to scorn. But when the people were put forth, He went in, and took her by the hand, and the maid arose.

Matthew 9:23-25

While He was still speaking, a man from the house of the director of the synagogue came and said [to Jairus], "Your daughter is dead; do not weary *and* trouble the Teacher any further." But Jesus, on hearing this, answered him, "Do not be seized with alarm *or* struck with fear; **simply believe** [in Me as able to do this], and she shall be made well." *{Fear changes your expectation.}*

Luke 8:49, 50 AMP

And He took the damsel by the hand, and said unto her, "Talitha cumi;" which is, being interpreted, "Damsel, I say unto thee, 'Arise.'" And straightway the damsel arose, and walked; for she was of the age of twelve years. And they were astonished with a great astonishment.

Mark 5:41, 42

(Healing of the blind men:) "...Do you believe that I am able to do this?" They said to Him, "Yes, Lord." Then He touched their eyes, saying, "According to your **faith** *and* trust *and* reliance [on the power invested in Me] be it done to you;" And their eyes were opened.

Matthew 9:28-30a AMP

But so much the more went there a fame abroad of Him: and great multitudes came together to hear, and to be healed by Him of their infirmities.

Luke 5:15

And they brought to Him a man who was deaf and had difficulty in speaking, and they begged Jesus to place His hand upon him. ...He said, "Ephphatha," which means, "Be opened!" And his ears were opened, his tongue was loosed, and he began to speak distinctly... And they were overwhelmingly astonished, saying, He has done everything excellently (commendably and nobly)! He even makes the deaf to hear and the dumb to speak!" *{The people acted on their faith.}*

Mark 7:32, 34, 35, 37 AMP

And He cometh to Bethsaida; and they bring a blind man unto Him, and besought Him to touch him. And He took the blind man by the hand, and led him out of the town; and when He had spit on his eyes, and put His hands upon him, He asked him if he saw ought. And he looked up, and said, "I see men as trees, walking." After that He put His hands again upon his eyes, and made him look up: and he was restored, and saw every man clearly.

Mark 8:22-25

And He was casting out a devil, and it was dumb. And it came to pass, when the devil was gone out, the dumb spake; and the people wondered.

Luke 11:14

As they went out, behold, they brought to Him a dumb man possessed with a devil. And when the devil was cast out, the dumb spake: and the multitudes marvelled, saying, "It was never so seen in Israel."

Matthew 9:32, 33

(Woman with demon-possessed daughter who said that even dogs eat the crumbs:) Then Jesus answered her, "O woman, great is your faith! Be it done for you as you wish." And her daughter was cured from that moment.

Matthew 15:28 AMP

A.D.D. Healed

"I have struggled with memory retention problems all my life, and it has been especially frustrating whenever I tried to memorize Scripture. It was an impossible task for me. As hard as I would try, I could never do it. About eight years ago, I finally went to a doctor about my retention and memory concerns. He told me that I had A.D.D. He put me on Ritalin, and I had some measure of success for a while. After a few months, the Ritalin no longer seemed to have any affect on me, so I quit taking it.

"About six months ago, I went to a teaching on healing by Nancy Insley and was prayed for to receive healing of the A.D.D. The following day, I decided to put the healing to the test while I was shopping for groceries. As I walked down the aisle, I asked God to bring Scriptures to my mind by using grocery items as a trigger. The first item I saw was a bottle of vinegar. Suddenly the Scripture 'They also gave Me gall for My food, and for My thirst they gave Me vinegar to drink' came to mind. Next, I went to the detergent aisle. When I saw the bottle of Gain, the Scripture 'I count all things lost that I might gain Christ' popped into my mind. Then when I noticed the Angel Soft bath tissue, another Scripture came to me: 'And behold an angel of the Lord appeared to them saying, "Do not be afraid, for behold I bring you tidings of great joy, For unto you this day is born in the city of David, a Savior, who is Christ the Lord."' After that, I walked over to the insect repellents. As I looked at a picture of a dead cockroach on a can of Raid, the verses came to mind that tell us that Christ came to destroy every work of the enemy and how

we, the church, are called to raid the enemy's camp and to take back what he has stolen.

"Needless to say, it was the best day I had ever had at the grocery store, and I praise God for my healing!"—Chris

And she answered and said unto Him, "Yes, Lord: yet the dogs under the table eat of the children's crumbs." And He said unto her, "For this saying go thy way; the devil is gone out of thy daughter." And when she was come to her house, she found the devil gone out, and her daughter laid upon the bed.

Mark 7:28-30

And certain women, which had been <u>healed</u> of evil spirits and infirmities, Mary called Magdalene, out of whom went seven devils,

Luke 8:2

Now when Jesus was risen early the first day of the week, He appeared first to Mary Magdalene, out of whom He had cast seven devils.

Mark 16:9

(Demon-possessed Gadarene:) They also which saw it told them by what means he that was possessed of the devils was <u>healed</u>.

Luke 8:36

And they come to Jesus, and see him that was possessed with the devil, and had the legion, sitting, and clothed, and in his right mind: and they were afraid.

Mark 5:15

And when He had called unto Him His twelve disciples, He gave them power against unclean spirits, to cast them out, and to heal all manner of sickness and all manner of disease.

Matthew 10:1

"Heal the sick, cleanse the lepers, raise the dead, cast out devils: freely ye have received, freely give."

Matthew 10:8

Then Jesus called together the Twelve [apostles] and gave them power and authority over **all** demons, and to cure diseases, And He sent them out to announce *and* preach the kingdom of God, and to bring healing.

Luke 9:1, 2 AMP

And they departed, and went through the towns, preaching the Gospel, and healing **every where**.

Luke 9:6

And He called unto Him the twelve, and began to send them forth by two and two; and gave them power over unclean spirits; And they cast out many devils, and anointed with oil many that were sick, and healed them.

Mark 6:7, 13

(Jesus commanded the seventy disciples whom He sent out:) "And heal the sick that are therein, and say unto them, 'The kingdom of God is come nigh unto you.'" *{Miraculous healing is a sign that the Kingdom of God is at hand.}*

Luke 10:9

(Blind man; Jesus made mud for his eyes:) "Go, wash in the Pool of Siloam—which means Sent." So he went and washed, and came back seeing. *{This man had enough faith to do as Jesus commanded and to wash the mud off.}*

John 9:7 AMP

And it is easier for heaven and earth to pass, than one tittle of the law to fail. *{God's Word is true. If He says that by His stripes you were healed, then you were!}*

Luke 16:17

"And ye shall know the Truth, and the Truth shall make you free." *{This means free from sickness, sin, curses, etc.}*

John 8:32

...and when Jesus saw their **faith**, He said to the paralyzed man, "Take courage, son; your sins are forgiven *and* the penalty remitted" "But in order that you may know that the Son of Man has authority on earth to forgive sins *and* remit the penalty," He then said to the paralyzed man, "Get up! Pick up your sleeping pad and go to your own house." When the crowds saw it, they were struck with fear *and* awe; and they recognized God *and* praised *and* thanked Him, Who had given such power *and* authority to men.

Matthew 9:2, 6, 8 AMP

(Paralytic on stretcher:) And when He saw **their faith**, He said unto him, "Man, thy sins are forgiven thee." "Whether is easier, to say, 'Thy sins be forgiven thee;' or to say, 'Rise up and walk'? But that ye may know that the Son of man hath power upon earth to forgive sins," (He said unto the sick of the palsy,) "I say unto thee, 'Arise, and take up thy couch, and go into thine house.'" *{Sin and sickness are from the devil; the forgiveness of sin and health are part of our salvation "package".}*

Luke 5:20, 23, 24

And, behold, there was a certain man before Him which had the dropsy. And Jesus answering spake unto the lawyers and Pharisees, saying, "Is it lawful to heal on the sabbath day?" And they held their peace. And He took him, and healed him, and let him go;

Luke 14:2-4

And there was a woman there who for eighteen years had had an infirmity caused by a **spirit** (a **demon of sickness**). She was bent completely forward and utterly unable to straighten herself up *or* to look upward. And when Jesus saw her, He called [her to Him] and said to her, "Woman, you are <u>released</u> from your infirmity!"

Luke 13:11, 12 AMP

(Ten healed of leprosy:) And when He saw them, He said to them, "Go [at once] and show yourselves to the priests." And as they went, they were cured *and* made clean.

Luke 17:14 AMP

(Paralytic on stretcher:) When Jesus saw their **faith**... [He said,] "Arise, and take up thy bed, and go thy way into thine house." And immediately he arose, took up the bed, and went forth before them all; insomuch that they were all amazed, and glorified God, saying, "We never saw it on this fashion."

Mark 2:5, 11, 12

And, behold, there came a leper and worshiped Him, saying, "Lord, if Thou wilt, Thou canst make me clean." And Jesus put forth His hand, and touched him, saying, "I will; be thou clean." And immediately his leprosy was cleansed.

Matthew 8:2, 3

And it came to pass, when He was in a certain city, behold a man full of leprosy: who seeing Jesus fell on his face, and besought Him, saying, "Lord, if Thou wilt, Thou canst make me clean." And He put forth His hand, and touched him, saying, "<u>I will</u>: be thou clean." And immediately the leprosy departed from him. *{The leper clearly had faith.}*

Luke 5:12, 13

And a leper came to Him, begging Him on his knees and saying to Him, "If You are willing, You are able to make me clean." And being moved with pity *and* sympathy, Jesus reached out His hand and touched him, and said to him, "I am willing; be made clean!" And at once the leprosy [completely] left him and he was made clean [by being healed]. *{The leper had faith in the Word of Jesus.}*

Mark 1:40-42 AMP

And a certain man lame from his mother's womb was carried, whom they laid daily at the gate of the temple which is called Beautiful, to ask alms of them that entered into the temple; Who seeing Peter and John about to go into the temple asked an alms. And Peter, fastening his eyes upon him with John, said, "Look on us." And he gave heed unto them, expecting to receive something of them. Then Peter said, "Silver and gold have I none; but such as I have give I thee: In the name of Jesus Christ of Nazareth rise up and walk." And he took him by the right hand, and lifted him up: and immediately his feet and ankle bones received strength. And he leaping up stood, and walked, and entered with them into the temple, walking, and leaping, and praising God.

Acts 3:2-8

"...by the Name of Jesus Christ of Nazareth, Whom ye crucified, Whom God raised from the dead, even by Him doth this man stand here before you whole."

Acts 4:10

And the people with one accord gave heed unto those things which Philip spake, hearing and seeing the miracles which he did. For unclean **spirits**, crying with loud voice, came out of many that were possessed with them: and many taken with palsies, and that were lame, were healed.

Acts 8:6, 7

And there he found a certain man named Aeneas, which had kept his bed eight years, and was sick of the palsy. And Peter said unto him, "Aeneas, Jesus Christ maketh thee whole: arise, and make thy bed." And <u>he arose immediately</u>.

Acts 9:33, 34

[Peter said to dead Dorcas:] "Tabitha, get up!" And she opened her eyes; and when she saw Peter, she raised herself and sat upright.

Acts 9:40 AMP

Now at Lystra a man sat who found it impossible to use his feet, for he was a cripple from birth and had never walked. He was listening to Paul as he talked, and [Paul] gazing intently at him and observing that <u>he</u> had **faith** to be healed, shouted at him, saying, "Stand erect on your feet!" And he leaped up and walked.

Acts 14:8-10 AMP

And there sat in a window a certain young man named Eutychus, being fallen into a deep sleep: and as Paul was long preaching, he sunk down with sleep, and fell down from the third loft, and was taken up dead. And Paul went down, and fell on him, and embracing him said, "Trouble not yourselves; for his life is in him." When he therefore was come up again, and had broken bread, and eaten, and talked a long while, even till break of day, so he departed. And they brought the young man alive, and were not a little comforted.

Acts 20:9-12

So that from his [Paul's] body were brought unto the sick handkerchiefs or aprons, and the diseases departed from them, and the evil spirits went out of them. *[The anointing of God is transferable.]*

Acts 19:12

for the joy of the LORD is your strength.

Nehemiah 8:10b

"Fear thou not; for I am with thee: be not dismayed; for I am thy God: I will strengthen thee; yea, I will help thee..."

Isaiah 41:10

"But they that wait upon the LORD shall renew their strength; they shall mount up with wings as eagles; they shall run, and not be weary; and they shall walk, and not faint."

Isaiah 40:31

But if the Spirit of Him that raised up Jesus from the dead dwell in you, He that raised up Christ from the dead shall also quicken your mortal bodies by His Spirit that dwelleth in you. *{"Quicken" means "to make alive".}*

Romans 8:11

Likewise the Spirit also helpeth our infirmities.

Romans 8:26

And the prayer [that is] of **faith** will save him who is sick, and the Lord will restore him; and if he has committed sins, he will be forgiven. Confess to one another therefore your faults (your slips, your false steps, your offenses, your sins) and pray [also] for one another, that you may be healed *and* restored... The earnest (heartfelt, continued) prayer of a righteous man makes tremendous power available [dynamic in its working]. *{Verse 14 asks, "Is anyone among you sick?" God's will is not for us to remain sick. The prayer of faith will make us whole.}*

James 5:15, 16 AMP

It is better to trust in the LORD than to put confidence in man. *{For example, doctors.}*

Psalm 118:8

And Asa in the thirty and ninth year of his reign was diseased in his feet, until his disease was exceeding great: yet <u>in his disease he sought **not** to the LORD</u>, but to the physicians. And Asa slept with his fathers, <u>and died</u> in the one and fortieth year of his reign.

2 Chronicles 16:12, 13

Many Broken Bones Healed

I have watched God heal many broken bones. After one of my meetings, a woman told me that she had come with a broken toe which was curled backwards and hanging off of her sandal. During the preaching, the toe slipped up into position and was fully restored!

In two different villages in the Philippines, two boys, each around one year of age, had broken arms that were instantaneously healed with the laying on of hands. Each of them excitedly started waving the arm around.

Two different ladies have come to meetings with broken backs. Both were instantly healed.

A man whose collarbone was broken was in great pain. He came forward for prayer and instantly, excitedly, threw up his arms, proclaiming his complete healing!

One lady in Croatia came up for neck and head pain from a broken neck due to an automobile accident. As soon as I laid my hand on her, she collapsed. Then she broke out in an immense grin, turning her head back and forth. She started exclaiming that all the pain was gone. She had felt a strength travel through her neck, and the pain had disappeared!

O Lord my God, I cried to You and You have healed me.
Psalm 30:2 AMP

...Thus saith the LORD, the God of David thy father, "I have heard thy prayer, I have seen thy tears: behold, I will heal thee... And I will add unto thy days fifteen years"
2 Kings 20:5, 6a

Blessed...is he who considers the weak *and* the poor... The Lord will sustain, refresh *and* strengthen him on his bed of languishing; all his bed You [O Lord] will turn, change, *and* transform in his illness.
Psalm 41:1a, 3 AMP

"I have seen his [willful] ways, but I will heal him."
Isaiah 57:18 AMP

"For I will restore health to you, and I will heal your wounds," says the Lord...
Jeremiah 30:17 AMP

And, behold, a woman, which was diseased with an issue of blood twelve years, came behind Him, and touched the hem of His garment: For she said within herself, "If I may but touch His garment, I shall be whole." But Jesus turned Him about, and when He saw her, He said, "Daughter, be of good comfort; thy faith hath made thee whole." And the woman was made whole from that hour.
Matthew 9:20-22

For she said, "If I may touch but His clothes, I shall be whole." And He said unto her, "Daughter, thy **faith** hath made thee whole; go in peace, and be whole of thy plague." *{Her confession and Jesus' response that her faith had made her whole uses the Greek word "sozo". This word means "to be healed, saved, delivered,*

protected, preserved and made whole". All these promises
we, too, received when we accepted Jesus as our Lord and
Savior.}

Mark 5:28, 34

And He said unto her, "Daughter, be of good comfort: thy
faith hath made thee whole; go in peace." *{Your faith will*
make you whole.}

Luke 8:48

"...turn again and be healed."

Isaiah 6:10 AMP

Trust in the LORD with all thine heart, and lean not unto
thine own understanding. In **all** thy ways acknowledge
Him, and He shall direct thy paths. Be not wise in thine
own eyes: fear the LORD, and depart from evil. It shall be
health to your navel *{body}*, and marrow *{refreshment or*
moistening} to thy bones.

Proverbs 3:5-8

"Behold, I am the LORD, the God of all flesh: is there
anything too hard for Me?"

Jeremiah 32:27

HEALING FOR ALL

Jesus Healed Them All

Jesus Christ the same yesterday, and to day, and for ever.

Bless the LORD, O my soul, and forget not all His benefits: Who forgiveth **all** thine iniquities; Who healeth **all** thy diseases;

Psalm 103:2, 3

(Referring to God bringing His people out of Egypt:) He brought them forth also with silver and gold, and there was **not one** <u>feeble</u> person among their tribes.

Psalm 105:37

He sent His Word, and healed them, and delivered them from their destructions. *{Jesus is the Word which was sent; He has already healed us.}*

Psalm 107:20

How God anointed Jesus of Nazareth with the Holy Ghost and with power: Who went about doing good, and **healing**

all that were oppressed of the devil; for God was with Him.

Acts 10:38

Surely He has borne our griefs (sicknesses, weaknesses, and distresses)... and with the stripes [that wounded] Him **we are healed *and* made whole**. *{He carried our pains and diseases for us. We <u>are</u> already healed and made whole!}*

Isaiah 53:4, 5 AMP

When evening came, they brought to Him many who were under the power of demons, and He drove out the spirits with a word, and restored to health **all** who were sick. And thus He fulfilled what was spoken by the prophet Isaiah, "He Himself took [in order to carry away] our weaknesses *and* infirmities and bore away our diseases." [Isa. 53:4.]

Matthew 8:16, 17 AMP

By His wounds you **have been** healed.

1 Peter 2:24b AMP

"And ye shall serve the LORD your God, and He shall bless thy bread, and thy water; and I will take sickness away from the midst of thee."

Exodus 23:25

And the LORD said unto Moses, "Make thee a fiery serpent, and set it upon a pole: and it shall come to pass, that every one that is bitten, when he looketh upon it, shall <u>live</u>." And Moses made a serpent of brass, and put it upon a pole, and it came to pass, that if a serpent had bitten any man, when he beheld the serpent of brass, he <u>lived</u>. *{This is, of course, symbolic of Christ going to the cross for us. If we look to Him for healing, we, too, will be healed.}*

Numbers 21:8, 9

Who executes justice for the oppressed, Who gives food to the hungry. The Lord sets free the prisoners, The Lord opens the eyes of the blind, the Lord lifts up those who are bowed down, the Lord loves the [uncompromisingly] righteous (those upright in heart and in right standing with Him).

Psalm 146:7, 8 AMP

Policeman With Severe Neck Injury Healed

"On October 24, 1984, in a suburb of San Diego, California, as a young six-year police veteran, I stumbled upon a drug deal between three men outside of a Junior High school. Even though I radioed for assistance, my fellow officers were at least 15 minutes away, leaving me alone.

"As I attempted to take the three men into custody, one of them, unbeknownst to me, was under the influence of a combination of methamphetamine and PCP. This not only gave the man super strength, but made him impervious to pain and very paranoid. This suspect violently resisted being arrested, severely injuring me in the neck, right shoulder and back.

"The commotion drew a large crowd of curious children who had just been dismissed from school. This prevented me from being able to unholster my gun to stop the struggle. I was forced to fight for my life and suffer severe injuries as a result. The injuries ended my career as a law enforcement officer; because if I got injured again, I would most likely become a quadriplegic. As a side effect of the injury, I suffered massive migraine-like headaches. The doctors said that the injury was almost exactly like another case involving a steel worker at a construction site. He had kept himself from being killed by reaching out and grabbing a girder after falling several stories.

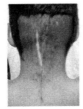 *"The massive headaches grew in frequency and severity over the next several years. The doctors were baffled as to how to help me. Finally, a leading neurosurgeon did surgery to sever nerves in the back of my neck near my spinal chord in an attempt to stop the pain signals from reaching the brain. While each new treatment helped for a time, the headache pain would eventually return as severe as before, if not worse. In addition, each treatment or surgery left its own side effect, complicating things even further.*

"My condition continued to worsen. The headache pain increased so severely, that my wife was frequently forced to take me to the emergency room, sometimes three or four times a week. The doctors finally decided that they could only treat the chronic headaches with powerful pain-killing medications. I was prescribed ever-increasingly high doses of Morphine each day to attempt to control the constant stabbing pain.

"The headache pain continued to increase in severity and frequency until finally, in 1994, I was unable to work any more. In May of 2003, Nancy and her husband came over and shared God's Truth on healing with us, showing us a number of Scriptures. They  *prayed with me, and I received my healing! Since then, I have been free of pain, weaned off the powerful pain killers, back to working full time and resumed my position of leading worship at church. Sing praises to the Name of the Lord most high, for He alone is worthy to be praised! Hallelujah!"—Ken*

"He giveth power to the faint; and to them that have no might He increaseth strength."

Isaiah 40:29

He healeth the broken in heart, and bindeth up their wounds. *{= heals their pains or wounds.}*

Psalm 147:3

...and they will return to the Lord, and He will listen to their entreaties and **heal** them.

Isaiah 19:22 AMP

[Jesus] went about...healing **every** disease and **every** weakness *and* infirmity among the people.

Matthew 4:23 AMP

...and they brought Him **all** who were sick, those afflicted with various diseases and torments, those under the power of demons, and epileptics, and paralyzed people, and He healed them.

Matthew 4:24 AMP

And Jesus went about all the cities and villages...curing **all** kinds of disease and **every** weakness *and* infirmity.

Matthew 9:35 AMP

Now when the sun was setting, **all** they that had any sick with divers diseases brought them unto Him; and He laid His hands on **every one** of them, and healed them.

Luke 4:40

But so much the more went there a fame abroad of Him: and great multitudes came together to hear, and to be healed by Him of their infirmities.

Luke 5:15

And when He had called unto Him His twelve disciples, He gave them **power** against unclean spirits, to cast them out, and to heal **all** manner of sickness and **all** manner of disease.

Matthew 10:1

"And as you go, preach, saying, 'The kingdom of heaven is at hand!' Cure the sick, raise the dead, cleanse the lepers, drive out demons. Freely (without pay) you have received, freely (without charge) give."

Matthew 10:7, 8 AMP

...and great multitudes followed Him, and He healed them **all**.

Matthew 12:15

And Jesus went forth, and saw a great multitude, and was moved with compassion toward them, and He healed their sick.

Matthew 14:14

And when the men of that place had knowledge of Him, they sent out into all that country round about, and brought unto Him **all that were diseased**; And besought Him that they might only touch the hem of His garment: and <u>as many as touched</u> were made perfectly whole. *{They put action to their faith.}*

Matthew 14:35, 36

And **great multitudes** came unto Him, having with them those that were lame, blind, dumb, maimed, and many others, and cast them down at Jesus' feet; and He healed them.

Matthew 15:30

And great multitudes followed Him, and He healed them there.

Matthew 19:2

And the blind and the lame came to Him in the temple; and He healed them.

Matthew 21:14

Our Son's Fatal Heart Condition Healed

"In 1985, our son, Andrew, was born with a major heart defect. As they laid him next to me on the hospital bed, I noticed that he was working far too hard for each breath. An EKG indicated that his heart was not functioning properly. The pediatric cardiologist was brought in, and he confirmed that something was very wrong with our son. We laid hands on our baby and prayed for him. A couple of days later, we took Andrew to the specialist's office, where he was examined using an ultrasound machine for the heart. We were allowed to be in the room and to watch the monitor screen. During the testing, the doctor remarked that the problem, which he had definitely detected and viewed on the readouts, had totally disappeared! He told us that our son was perfectly healthy, and that there was no need to ever bring him back into the office. The nurse followed us

out of the room and commented, 'I don't know if you understand the significance of what has just occurred: The surgeons can do so much to repair the heart nowadays, but the one chamber that your son had a defect in could not have been repaired. He would have died.' We praise our mighty God!"—Nancy Insley

And ran through that whole region round about, and began to carry about in beds those that were sick, where they heard He was. And whithersoever He entered, into villages, or cities, or country, they laid the sick in the streets, and besought Him that they might touch if it were but the border of His garment: and **as many as** touched Him were made whole. *{They came with expectation.}*

Mark 6:55, 56

"And these signs shall follow <u>them that **believe**</u>; In My Name shall they cast out devils; they shall speak with new tongues; they shall take up serpents; and if they drink any deadly thing, <u>it shall not hurt them</u>; they shall lay hands on the sick, and **they shall recover**." *{This is for all who believe!}*

Mark 16:17, 18

...who came to listen to Him and to be cured of their diseases—even those who were disturbed *and* troubled with unclean spirits, and they were being healed [also]. And **all** the multitude were seeking to touch Him, for healing power was all the while going forth from Him and curing them **all** [saving them from severe illnesses or calamities]. *{They had the faith to reach out to Him.}*

Luke 6:17-19 AMP

...and (Jesus) healed them that had need of healing.

Luke 9:11

And a great multitude followed Him, because they saw His miracles which He did on them that were diseased.

John 6:2

For He had healed so many that **all** who had distressing bodily diseases kept falling upon Him *and* pressing upon Him in order that they might touch Him. *{This demonstrates their faith and expectation.}*

Mark 3:10 AMP

And the people gathered also from the towns and hamlets around Jerusalem, bringing the sick and those troubled with foul **spirits** and they were **all** cured.

Acts 5:16 AMP

And it happened that the father of Publius was sick in bed with recurring attacks of fever and dysentery; and Paul went to see him, and after praying and laying his hands on him, he healed him. After this had occurred, the other people on the island who had diseases also kept coming and were cured. *{This does not indicate that only a couple were selectively healed, but that **all** of them were.}*

Acts 28:8, 9 AMP

Legs Grow Out; Hips Align

I have seen a large number of legs grow out or hips be aligned. One woman with hips out of alignment in Croatia was awakened in the night after I prayed with her. She testified that she could feel and hear the bones moving into position; and in the morning, her hips were straight.

Others can feel an adjustment taking place. When they get home and check, they find they have been supernaturally realigned.

Watching legs grow out is especially exciting. I do not know how He does it, but somehow God causes the bone to grow as well as the tendons, ligaments, skin, veins, etc. all to stretch or grow simultaneously. It always amazes me. We serve such a mighty, loving God!

And if you pour out that with which you sustain your own life for the hungry and satisfy the need of the afflicted...the Lord shall guide you continually and satisfy you in drought *and* in dry places and make strong your bones. And you shall be like a watered garden and like a spring of water whose waters fail not.

Isaiah 58:10, 11 AMP

(In caring for the poor:)...thine health shall spring forth speedily.

Isaiah 58:8a

Heal me, O Lord, and I shall be healed; save me and I shall be saved, for You are my praise.

Jeremiah 17:14 AMP

...let us hold fast our profession. For we have not an High Priest which cannot be touched with the feeling of our infirmities; but was in all points tempted like as we are, yet without sin. Let us therefore come boldly unto the throne of grace, that we may obtain mercy, and find grace to help in time of need. *{Jesus understands—He had the same temptations to be sick, but He did not sin; He resisted. In Him, we can find the grace to resist.}*

Hebrews 4:14b-16

You will guard him *and* keep him in perfect *and* constant peace whose mind...is stayed on You, because he commits himself to You, leans on You, *and* hopes confidently in You. *{"Peace" means "safe, well, happy, welfare, i.e. health, prosperity, peace, favour, great, (good) health, prosper(-ity, -ous)", and more according to Strong's Concordance, word 07965.}*

Isaiah 26:3 AMP

"Behold, ...I will lay upon it health and healing, and I will cure them and will reveal to them the abundance of peace (prosperity, security, stability) and truth."

Jeremiah 33:6 AMP

"Is not this the fast that I (God) have chosen? to loose the bands of wickedness, to undo the heavy burdens, and to let the oppressed go free, and that ye break every yoke?"

Isaiah 58:6

"...I have broken thy yoke, and burst thy bands..."

Jeremiah 2:20

Arthritis Healed

One lady had painful arthritis in her hip. When I laid my hand on her, she fell out under the power of God, much to the concern of the others, and was not conscious for 10-15 minutes. When she came to, she looked around surprised, shook her head, then had us help her up. She stood up, shook her head again, then, beaming from ear to ear, began dancing around exclaiming that all the pain was gone and that she was healed!

He has sent me to bind up *and* heal the brokenhearted, to proclaim **liberty** to the [physical and spiritual] captives and the opening of the prison *and* of the eyes to those who are **bound**.

Isaiah 61:1b AMP

"The Spirit of the Lord is upon Me, because He hath anointed Me to preach the Gospel to the poor; He hath sent Me to heal the brokenhearted, to preach deliverance to the captives, and recovering of sight to the blind, to set at liberty them that are bruised,"

Luke 4:18

FAITH VERSUS DOUBT

Our Faith Plays a Role in Healing

...there is no respect of persons (no partiality) with Him.

..."If thou canst believe, all things are possible to him that believeth."

Mark 9:23

I have strength for all things in Christ Who empowers me [I am ready for anything and equal to anything through Him Who infuses inner strength into me...].

Philippians 4:13 AMP

For with God nothing is ever impossible *and* no Word from God shall be without power *or* impossible of fulfillment.

Luke 1:37 AMP

...but he who believes in Him...shall not be put to shame *nor* be disappointed in his expectations.

Romans 9:33 AMP

For as he thinketh in his heart, so is he... *{If you see yourself as sick, you shall remain so. No matter what the words are that you are speaking, you will <u>be</u> as you truly <u>believe</u> yourself to be in your <u>heart</u>.}*

Proverbs 23:7

So then **faith** cometh by hearing, and hearing by the Word of God. *{Speaking God's Word will build your faith.}*

Romans 10:17

Yet we have the same <u>spirit of faith</u> as he had who wrote, "I have believed, and therefore have I spoken." We too believe, and therefore we speak. *{Speaking God's Word is a way to express our faith.}*

2 Corinthians 4:13 AMP

(Nobleman's son:) Jesus saith unto him, "Go thy way; thy son liveth." And the man <u>believed the Word that Jesus had spoken</u> unto him, and he went his way. And as he was now going down, his servants met him, and told him, saying, "Thy son liveth."

John 4:50, 51

And Simon answering said unto Him, "Master, we have toiled all the night, and have taken nothing: nevertheless <u>at Thy Word</u> I will let down the net." *{Taking Jesus at His Word will bring abundance in every area of our lives.}*

Luke 5:5

And Jesus answered them, "Truly I say to you, <u>if</u> you have **faith** (a firm relying trust) and **do not doubt**, you will not only do what has been done to the fig tree, but even if you <u>say</u> to this mountain, 'Be taken up and cast into the sea,' it will be done. And **whatever** you ask for in prayer, having **faith** *and* [really] believing, you will receive."

Matthew 21:21, 22 AMP

And Jesus, replying, said to them, "Have **faith** in God [constantly]. Truly I tell you, whoever says to this mountain, 'Be lifted up and thrown into the sea!' and **does not doubt** <u>at all</u> in his heart but **believes** that what he says will take place, <u>it will be done</u> for him. For this reason I am telling you, <u>whatever</u> you ask for in prayer, **believe** (trust and be confident) that it is granted to you, and <u>you will [get it]</u>."

Mark 11:22-24 AMP

"And these signs shall follow <u>them that **believe**</u>; In My Name shall they cast out devils; they shall speak with new tongues; they shall take up serpents; and if they drink any deadly thing, <u>it shall not hurt them</u>; they shall lay hands on the sick, and **they shall recover**." *{!!!! What tremendous promises and power!}*

Mark 16:17, 18

Broken Vertebra, Broken Foot and a Concussion

"Although very much out of character, Rachel's horse bucked her in February of 2008. Rachel, age 14, landed on her back and head on hard pavement. (Her ankle was already in a walking boot, having broken it when a horse slipped and fell on her.) She was taken to the emergency room where they took X-rays, did a CAT scan and an MRI. The doctor was sure that nothing was broken but confirmed that she had a severe concussion. Two days later, the hospital called to say that she had, indeed, broken a vertebra. She was advised to get to an orthopedist as quickly as possible. Rachel's mom made several calls, but no one would treat her due to her age and the length of time which had elapsed since the accident. Their only help could come from the original emergency room. A few days later, they were able to be seen and have more X-rays taken. The doctor said that more damage had been done to her back than they had

originally suspected.

"I was asked to give Rachel a call. After talking about what God's Word says about healing, I asked if she wanted prayer. She felt she was ready to receive healing. As I prayed with her over the phone, Rachel removed the braces from her back and her ankle (that is faith!). When asked if she had noticed anything, she exclaimed, 'Oh, my gosh, the pain is gone!' She stood up and was walking around. She was twisting and turning her broken ankle when suddenly I heard her cry out, 'Oh, my gosh, the swelling is gone! I can move it to the side and point my toes! Now, I am walking on it, and all the pain is gone!' When I asked how her back felt, she responded, 'It doesn't hurt at all, and I am not even wearing my brace!'

"Rachel felt so good that she cleaned the house and did all the laundry before her mom came home from work. After this, Rachel had the scheduled X-rays, CAT scan and MRI repeated at the Oregon Health and Sciences University Hospital. When the doctor called two days later with the report, he was unsure as to how to express himself. Hemming and hawing, he said, 'The X-rays are very reassuring: we see no break, and she no longer shows any signs of the concussion. Everything is normal. Well, ummmm, I don't know what else to tell you. How is the patient doing?' Her mom assured him that she was FREE of pain and wanting to ride her horse! He said, 'No, no, no! We just don't know!'"—As related by Rachel and her mom together with Nancy

"Rachel has remained pain-free, is back jumping her horses and is enjoying life again!"—Rachel's mom

For He had healed so many that **all** who had distressing bodily diseases kept falling upon Him *and* pressing upon Him in order that they might touch Him. *{This demonstrates their faith and expectation.}*

Mark 3:10 AMP

And the apostles said unto the Lord, "Increase our faith." And the Lord said, "If ye had **faith** as a grain of mustard seed, ye might say unto this sycamine tree, 'Be thou plucked up by the root, and be thou planted in the sea'; and it should obey you." *{We must increase our own faith by hearing the Word, aligning our thinking with the Word of God and speaking out His Truths.}*

Luke 17:5, 6

Now faith is the substance of things hoped for, the evidence of things <u>not seen</u>. *{"Hoped for" means "confidently expected". In the same way that we have faith to believe in Jesus, Whom we cannot see, we must believe in and <u>expect</u> our healing <u>before</u> we see it. Our faith (assurance) changes into reality what we confidently expect. Faith brings us through to the victory.}*

Hebrews 11:1

While we look not at the things which are seen, but at the things which are not seen: for the things which are seen are temporal; but the things which are not seen are eternal. *{A promise of God, like healing, may not yet be seen; but **faith** believes an eternal promise <u>before</u> it is seen in this natural realm.}*

2 Corinthians 4:18

Through **faith** we understand that the worlds were framed by the Word of God, so that things which are seen were not made of things which do appear. *{"Which do appear" means "which are visible". The Word of God works in the*

spiritual realm. Our faith will work in the spiritual realm to cause the unseen, like health, to appear.}
Hebrews 11:3

Whom having not seen, ye love; in Whom, though now ye see Him not, yet believing, ye rejoice with joy unspeakable and full of glory: *{See comment above for Hebrews 11:1.}*
1 Peter 1:8

For in [this] hope we were saved. But hope [the object of] which is seen is not hope. For how can one hope for what he already sees? But if we hope for what is still unseen by us, we wait for it with patience *and* composure. *{"Hope" means "confident expectation". "Saved" here is "sozo" which can be translated "healed" or "to be made whole": "For in confident expectation, we were saved, healed and made whole."}*
Romans 8:24, 25 AMP

For we walk by **faith** [we regulate our lives and conduct ourselves by our conviction or belief respecting man's relationship to God and divine things, with trust and holy fervor; thus we walk] not by sight *or* appearance. *{We must walk by faith and not let the appearance of symptoms cause doubt nor fear. Our faith must look at God's divine Truth. Feelings having nothing to do with faith.}*
2 Corinthians 5:7 AMP

Let us hold fast the profession of our faith **without wavering**; (for He is **faithful** that promised).
Hebrews 10:23

Do not, therefore, fling away your fearless confidence, for it carries a great *and* glorious compensation of reward. For you have need of steadfast patience *and* endurance, so that you may perform *and* **fully** accomplish the will of God, and thus receive *and* carry away [and enjoy to the full] what is promised. *{Do not give up; endure until you are healed!}*

Hebrews 10:35, 36 AMP

One-Legged Knee Bends

In Germany, one young man, glowing with the love of God, came up for prayer for various problems after the preaching. He asked for prayer for a knee that had been injured and that he was no longer able to put a lot of weight on. As he returned to his seat, he kept pausing to do <u>one-legged</u> knee bends with the knee that had been hurting him! The following morning, he testified that the chronic stuffiness and drippy nose we had prayed about had also been totally healed.

In Madagascar, one older gentleman also had knee problems. After I laid my hand on his knee, he boldly tested the leg, even going so far as to jumping up and landing only on the formerly-bad leg a few times. He was joyous over his healing.

For by [**faith**—trust and holy fervor born of faith] the men of old had divine testimony borne to them *and* obtained a good report. *{By faith, God's approval was won.}*

Hebrews 11:2 AMP

But without **faith** it is impossible to please Him (God): ...He is a Rewarder of them that diligently seek Him. *{Sickness is <u>not</u> a reward.}*

Hebrews 11:6

...he who **believes** in Him...shall never be disappointed *or* put to shame.

1 Peter 2:6 AMP

"As I was with Moses, so I will be with thee: I will not fail thee, nor forsake thee." *{Trust God; He will not let you down.}*

Joshua 1:5b AMP

Through **faith** also Sara herself received strength to conceive seed, and was delivered of a child when she was past age, because <u>she judged Him faithful</u> Who had promised.

Hebrews 11:11

So then, those who are people of **faith** are blessed *and* made happy *and* favored by God...

Galatians 3:9a AMP

Know *and* understand that it is [really] the people [who live] by **faith** who are [the true] sons of Abraham.

Galatians 3:7 AMP

...(F)or the Scripture says, "The man in right standing with God [the just, the righteous] shall live by *and* out of **faith**, *and* he who through *and* by faith is declared righteous *and* in right standing with God shall live."

Galatians 3:11 AMP

...but the just shall live by his **faith**.

Habakkuk 2:4

Therefore take up the whole armor of God, that you may be able to withstand in the evil day, and having done all, to stand.

Ephesians 6:13

Above all, taking the shield of **faith**, wherewith ye shall be able to quench **all** the fiery darts of the wicked. And take the helmet of salvation, and the sword of the Spirit, which is the Word of God:

Ephesians 6:16, 17

Fight the good fight of faith, lay hold on eternal life, whereunto thou art also called, and hast professed a good profession before many witnesses. *{A good profession will agree with the Word of God.}*

1 Timothy 6:12a

For ever, O LORD, Thy Word is settled in heaven.

Psalm 119:89

Thy Word is very pure: therefore Thy servant loveth it.

Psalm 119:140

You will guard him *and* keep him in perfect *and* constant peace whose mind...is stayed on You, because he commits himself to You, leans on You, *and* hopes confidently in You. *{"Peace" means "safe, well, happy, welfare, i.e. health, prosperity, peace, favour, great, (good) health, prosper(-ity, -ous)", and more according to Strong's Concordance, word 07965.}*

Isaiah 26:3 AMP

For the Word that God speaks is alive and full of **power** [making it active, operative, energizing, and effective]... *{Put your faith in the Word that God has spoken. The power resident within His Word will heal you and change situations!}*

Hebrews 4:12a AMP

And the prayer [that is] of **faith** will save him who is sick, and the Lord will restore him; and if he has committed sins, he will be forgiven. Confess to one another therefore your faults (your slips, your false steps, your offenses, your sins) and pray [also] for one another, <u>that you may be healed</u> *and* restored... The earnest (heartfelt, continued) prayer of a righteous man makes <u>tremendous power</u> available [dynamic in its working]. *{Verse 14 asks, "Is <u>anyone</u> among you sick?" God's will is not for us to <u>remain</u> sick. The prayer of faith will make us whole.}*

James 5:15, 16 AMP

That if thou shalt confess with thy mouth the Lord Jesus, and shalt **believe** in thine heart... *{We must confess what we believe—not the problem!}*

Romans 10:9

Inordinately Long List of Ailments

I have prayed with a number of individuals who have suffered an inordinately long list of ailments. What a joy it is to see them healed of everything! All pain leaves! All symptoms leave! The doctors are absolutely amazed when they re-examine these patients. (See Appendix.)

For with the <u>heart</u> a person believes (adheres to, trusts in, and relies on Christ) and so is justified (declared righteous, acceptable to God), and with the mouth he confesses (declares openly and speaks out freely his **faith**) *and* confirms [his] **salvation**. *{"Salvation" means "rescue or safety, deliver, health, salvation, save, saving" according to Strong's Concordance, word 4991.}*

Romans 10:10 AMP

Let us draw near with a true heart in full **assurance** of faith, having our hearts sprinkled from an evil conscience, and our bodies washed with pure water.

Hebrews 10:22

It is because of the Lord's mercy *and* loving-kindness that we are not consumed, because His [tender] compassions fail not. They are new every morning; great *and* abundant is Your stability *and* faithfulness. "The Lord is my portion *or* share," says my living being (my inner self); "therefore will I hope in Him *and* wait expectantly for Him." The Lord is good to those who wait hopefully *and* expectantly for Him, to those who seek Him...

Lamentations 3:22-25 AMP

It is better to trust in the LORD than to put confidence in man. *{For example, doctors.}*

Psalm 118:8

And set your minds *and* keep them set on what is above (the higher things), not on the things that are on the earth. *{What has God said in His Word? Keep your mind on that and not on the problem.}*

Colossians 3:2 AMP

This is my comfort *and* consolation in my affliction: that Your Word has revived me *and* given me **life**.

Psalm 119:50 AMP

...revive *and* stimulate me according to Your Word!

Psalm 119:25b AMP

"...I have set before you life and death, blessing and cursing: therefore choose life, that both thou and thy seed may live:" *{We make the choice. In faith, choose to live.}*

Deuteronomy 30:19

"It is the Spirit Who gives life [He is the Life-giver;]...The words (truths) that I have been speaking to you are spirit and life. But [still] some of you fail to **believe** *and* **trust** *and* have **faith**."

John 6:63, 64a AMP

89

The entrance of Thy words giveth light; it giveth understanding unto the simple.

Psalm 119:130

Howbeit many of them which heard the Word **believed**. *{In this case, the Word was Jesus Himself. Jesus says at least six times, "He that hath ears to hear, let him hear." Hear the Word of God, believe It and speak It.}*

Acts 4:4

For in the Gospel a righteousness which God ascribes is revealed, both springing from **faith** and leading to **faith** [disclosed through the way of faith that arouses to more faith]. As it is written, "The man who through **faith** is just *and* upright shall live *and* shall live by **faith**." [Hab. 2:4]

Romans 1:17 AMP

(Jairus) begged Him earnestly, saying, "My little daughter is at the point of death. Come and lay Your hands on her, so that she may be healed *and* live." *{Jairus had great faith.}*

Mark 5:23 AMP

While He was still speaking, a man from the house of the director of the synagogue came and said [to Jairus], "Your daughter is dead; do not weary *and* trouble the Teacher any further." But Jesus, on hearing this, answered him, "Do not be seized with alarm *or* struck with fear; **simply believe** [in Me as able to do this], and she shall be made well." *{Fear changes your expectation.}*

Luke 8:49, 50 AMP

(To Jairus:) ..."Do not be seized with alarm *and* struck with fear; only **keep on believing**." *{Jesus is saying, "Just because there was a change in the circumstances, do not give up the great faith that you had."}*

Mark 5:36 AMP

But the centurion replied to Him, "Lord, I am not worthy *or* fit to have You come under my roof; but only speak the word, and my servant boy will be cured." "...I have not found so much **faith** as this with anyone, even in Israel." Then to the centurion Jesus said, "Go; it shall be done for you as you have believed." And the servant boy was restored to health at that very moment.

Matthew 8:8, 10, 13 AMP

Lice Dies Instantly

"Six-year-old Emily came home from school with lice. My daughter examined her scalp, and she could see that it was wriggling with lice. The child said to call me, and then she would be healed. God is pleased with such faith. We prayed over the phone, and the lice instantly died. There were no more lice to be seen, the nit comb picked up nothing more, and all the itching had stopped. Praise God!"—Nancy Insley

"But [just] speak a word, and my servant boy **will be healed**"... Now when Jesus heard this, He marveled at him, and He turned and said to the crowd that followed Him, "I tell you, not even in [all] Israel have I found such **great faith** [as this]." And when the messengers...returned to the house, they found the bond servant *who had been ill* quite well again. *{There are degrees of faith released: great faith, much faith, little faith and no faith.}*

Luke 7:7b, 9, 10 AMP

(Woman with demon-possessed daughter who said that even dogs eat the crumbs:) Then Jesus answered her, "O woman, **great** is your **faith**! Be it done for you as you wish." And her daughter was cured from that moment.

Matthew 15:28 AMP

(Ten healed of leprosy:) And when He saw them, He said to them, "Go [at once] and show yourselves to the priests." And as they went, they were cured *and* made clean. *{They showed faith <u>before</u> results were seen.}* Then one of them, upon seeing that he was cured, turned back, recognizing *and* thanking *and* praising God with a loud voice... And He said to him, "Get up and go on your way. Your **faith** (your trust and confidence that spring from your belief in God) has restored you to health."

Luke 17:14, 15, 19 AMP

Now at Lystra a man sat who found it impossible to use his feet, for he was a cripple from birth and had never walked. He was listening to Paul as he talked, and [Paul] gazing intently at him and observing that <u>he</u> had **faith** to be healed, shouted at him, saying, "Stand erect on your feet!" And he leaped up and walked.

Acts 14:8-10 AMP

(Gate Beautiful in Jerusalem:) "And His Name through **faith** in His Name hath made this man strong, whom ye see and know: yea, the **faith** which is by Him hath given him this perfect soundness in the presence of you all."

Acts 3:16

(God speaking to Abraham:) ..."Look now toward heaven, and tell the stars, if thou be able to number them:" and He said unto him, "So shall thy seed be." And he <u>believed</u> in the LORD; and He counted it to him for righteousness. *{Abraham stood strong in his faith despite the natural circumstances.}*

Genesis 15:5, 6

(As it is written, "I have made thee a father of many nations,") before Him whom he believed, even God, who quickeneth the dead, and <u>calleth those things which be not as though they were</u>. Who against hope believed in hope, that he might become the father of many nations, <u>according to that which was spoken</u>, "So shall thy seed be." And **being not weak in faith**, he considered **not** his own body now dead, when he was about an hundred years old, neither yet the deadness of Sara's womb: He **staggered not** at the promise of God through **unbelief**; but was <u>strong</u> in **faith**, giving glory to God; and <u>being fully persuaded</u> that, what He had promised, He was able also to perform. And therefore it was imputed to him for righteousness. *{We are not to consider the circumstances, but to trust in Him and to speak what God would speak. (See also the comment for Romans 4:17 under "The Importance of Our Words".)}*

Romans 4:17-22

And so, after he (Abraham) had patiently endured, he obtained the promise. *{If we will patiently endure, we will obtain the promise of healing.}*

Hebrews 6:15

That ye be not slothful, but followers of them who through **faith** and patience inherit the promises.

Hebrews 6:12

(Paralytic on stretcher:) And when He saw **their faith**, He said unto him, "Man, thy sins are forgiven thee." "Whether is easier, to say, 'Thy sins be forgiven thee;' or to say, 'Rise up and walk'? But that ye may know that the Son of man hath power upon earth to forgive sins," (He said unto the sick of the palsy,) "I say unto thee, 'Arise, and take up thy couch, and go into thine house.'" *{Sin and sickness are from the devil; the forgiveness of sin and health are part of our salvation "package".}*

Luke 5:20, 23, 24

(Paralytic on stretcher:) ...and when Jesus saw their **faith,** He said to the paralyzed man, "Take courage, son; your sins are forgiven *and* the penalty remitted" "But in order that you may know that the Son of Man has authority on earth to forgive sins *and* remit the penalty," He then said to the paralyzed man, "Get up! Pick up your sleeping pad and go to your own house." When the crowds saw it, they were struck with fear *and* awe; and they recognized God *and* praised *and* thanked Him, Who had given such power *and* authority to men.

Matthew 9:2, 6, 8 AMP

(Paralytic on stretcher:) When Jesus saw their **faith...** [He said,] "Arise, and take up thy bed, and go thy way into thine house."

Mark 2:5, 11

(Bleeding woman:)...He said, "Take courage, daughter! Your **faith** has made you well..."

Matthew 9:22 AMP

(Bleeding woman:) For she said, "If I may touch but His clothes, I shall be whole." And He said unto her, "Daughter, thy **faith** hath made thee whole; go in peace, and be whole of thy plague."

Mark 5:28, 34

(Bleeding woman:) And He said unto her, "Daughter, be of good comfort: thy **faith** hath made thee whole; go in peace."

Luke 8:48

(Ruler's dead daughter:) And when Jesus came into the ruler's house, and saw the minstrels and the people making a noise, He said unto them, "Give place: for the maid is not dead, but sleepeth." And they laughed Him to scorn. But when the people were put forth, He went in, and took her by the hand, and the maid arose. *[Jesus was speaking faith and was not moved by the circumstances. The people scorned Him for it. Once He removed the **unbelief** and **doubt** from the room, the power of faith was able to flow and to perform its work.]*

Matthew 9:23-25

(Healing of the blind men:) When He reached the house and went in, the blind men came to Him, and Jesus said to them, "Do you believe that I am able to do this?" They said to Him, "Yes, Lord." Then He touched their eyes, saying, "According to your **faith** *and* trust *and* reliance [on the power invested in Me] be it done to you;" And their eyes were opened.

Matthew 9:28-30a AMP

And ran through that whole region round about, and began to carry about in beds those that were sick, where they heard He was. And whithersoever He entered, into villages, or cities, or country, they laid the sick in the streets, and besought Him that they might touch if it were but the border of His garment: and as many as touched Him were made whole. *[They came with expectation.]*

Mark 6:55, 56

...and He said to the man with the withered hand, "Come and stand here in the midst." And he arose and stood there. ...[Jesus] said to the man, "Stretch out your hand!" And he did so, and his hand was fully restored *like the other one.*

Luke 6:8, 10 AMP

(Man with withered hand:) ...and [Jesus] said to the man, "Hold out your hand." He held it out, and his hand was [completely] restored.

Mark 3:5 AMP

(Man with withered hand:) Then He said to the man, "Reach out your hand." And the man reached it out and it

95

was restored, as sound as the other one. *{He acted on his faith in Jesus.}*

Matthew 12:13 AMP

Acting On Your Faith

Very often, I see that folks receive their healing when they are willing to step out and to act on their faith. I will often encourage them to move what they could not move before or do something that had previously caused them pain. They quickly find that they are able to raise their arms high above their heads, bend over, twist around, do knee bends, or whatever else they could not do before. The injured areas get loosened up, strengthened and healed.

One teenager had had swollen feet and ankles for years. After prayer, God instructed that she run around outside. When she came back in, she was healed!

(Lame man at pool of Bethesda:) When Jesus noticed him lying there [helpless], knowing that he had already been a long time in that condition, He said to him, "Do you want to become well? [Are you really in earnest about getting well?]" Jesus said to him, "Get up! Pick up your bed (sleeping pad) and walk!" Instantly the man became well *and* recovered his strength and picked up his bed and walked. *{The man responded in faith by rising up.}*

John 5:6, 8, 9a AMP

(Blind Bartimaeus:) And Jesus said to him, "Go your way; your **faith** has healed you." And at once he received his sight and accompanied Jesus on the road.

Mark 10:52 AMP

And Jesus said to him, "Receive your sight! Your **faith** (your trust and confidence that spring from your faith in God) has healed you."

Luke 18:42 AMP

And there he found a certain man named Aeneas, which had kept his bed eight years, and was sick of the palsy. And Peter said unto him, "Aeneas, Jesus Christ maketh thee whole: arise, and make thy bed." And <u>he arose immediately</u>. *{Note: "maketh thee whole" is using the Greek middle voice. "This voice means that the SUBJECT **initiates** the action and **participates** in the results of the action. The middle voice indicates the subject performs an action upon himself or herself (reflexive action) or <u>for their own benefit</u>."[1] Jesus is the "subject" who performs the healing for His own benefit! Aeneas had enough faith to believe this, so he was able to accept the Truth and to be healed.}*

Acts 9:33, 34

Take heed, brethren, lest there be in any of you an evil heart of **unbelief,**

Hebrews 3:12a

For unto us was the Gospel preached, as well as unto them: but the word preached did not profit them, not being mixed with **faith** in them that heard it. *{A part of the Gospel is our healing. Mix faith with what you are reading now.}*

Hebrews 4:2

For whatsoever is born of God overcometh the world: and this is the victory that overcometh the world, even our **faith**. *{We overcome the devil, who is the god of this world, through our faith in the Word of God.}*

1 John 5:4

---

[1] Greek Quick Reference Guide on http://www.preceptaustin.org//new_page_40.htm

Seeing therefore it remaineth that some must enter therein, and they to whom it was first preached entered not in because of **unbelief**:

Hebrews 4:6

Let us labour therefore to enter into that rest, lest any man fall after the same example of **unbelief**.

Hebrews 4:11

For whatever does not originate *and* proceed from **faith** is sin [whatever is done without a conviction of its approval by God is sinful]. *{Complaining, talking the problem, and lack of faith towards healing is sin.}*

Romans 14:23b AMP

But without **faith** it is impossible to please Him (God):

Hebrews 11:6

But let endurance *and* steadfastness *and* patience have full play *and* do a thorough work, so that you may be [people] perfectly and fully developed [with no defects], lacking in nothing.
Only it must be in **faith** that he asks with no wavering (no hesitating, no doubting). For the one who wavers (hesitates, doubts) is like the billowing surge out at sea that is blown hither *and* thither and tossed by the wind. For truly, let not such a person imagine that he will receive anything [he asks for] from the Lord.
[For being as he is] a man of two minds (hesitating, dubious, irresolute), [he is] unstable *and* unreliable *and* uncertain about everything [he thinks, feels, decides].

James 1:4, 6-8 AMP

He shall not be afraid of evil tidings: his heart is fixed, **trusting** in the LORD. *{Evil tidings include negative reports from the doctor.}*

Psalm 112:7

"And blessed is he, whosoever shall not be offended in Me." *{or* "shall find no occasion of stumbling in Me" *(American Standard Version) or* "who has <u>no doubts</u> about Me" *(Bible in Basic English). We <u>will</u> experience His blessings if we will not doubt Him or His Word.}*

Luke 7:23

"Now the just shall live by **faith**: but if any man <u>draw back</u>, My soul shall have <u>no pleasure</u> in him."

Hebrews 10:38

What time I am afraid, I will have **confidence** in *and* put my **trust** *and* reliance in You. By [the help of] God I will praise His Word; on God I lean, rely, *and* confidently put my trust; I will not fear.

Psalm 56:3, 4a AMP

The LORD is on my side; I will not fear...

Psalm 118:6

For God hath not given us the spirit of fear; but of power, and of love, and of a sound mind. *{We must not let fear or doubt keep us from bringing God glory through the power He has placed in us for healing. Satan wants to hinder God's work in and through us, but faith conquers fear. Faith is the opposite of fear.}*

2 Timothy 1:7

The Lord is my Light and my Salvation—whom shall I fear *or* dread? The Lord is the Refuge *and* Stronghold of my life—of whom shall I be afraid? For in the day of trouble He will hide me in His shelter... Teach me Your way, O Lord, and lead me in a plain *and* even path...

Psalm 27:1, 5, 11 AMP

"My Hips Were Out of Alignment"

"For many years, I had suffered with lower back and hip pain. At times, it became so unbearable that I couldn't even sit in church for an hour without being so miserable and uncomfortable that I would have to reposition myself over and over again. Nothing I did seemed to help very much. It was difficult to find any position that I could be comfortable in for any length of time, even to sleep. I tried a series of physical therapy treatments and exercises, but all seemed to bring just a temporary relief.

"I began to notice that when looking in the mirror straight on, I could actually see that my hips were out of alignment by maybe as much as an inch. I knew I could be healed by the power of God and had prayed for myself and had also been prayed for by others. Then one day, when Nancy and I were in a restaurant having lunch, I began to share the problem with her. She said, 'Let's just agree for healing right now.'

"We stood up, and after she prayed with me, she asked me to do something I couldn't do before. I bent over and touched my toes several times. Then she asked me if the pain was gone. I said that it was better but not entirely gone, so she laid hands on me again. The pain left completely! When I got home and checked in the mirror, I could see that my hips were now properly aligned!

"I'm so thankful that she was persistent and for the faithfulness of our precious Lord and Savior! I am now in perfect alignment and have been free of pain for three years. I had forgotten how good it feels to feel good! Praise God!"—Julie

(Peter walking on the water:) Instantly Jesus reached out His hand and caught *and* held him, saying to him, "O, you of **little** faith, why did you doubt?" *{Peter was successful until doubt and fear crept in, bringing his downfall (i.e. sinking).}*

Matthew 14:31 AMP

"...O, ye of **little faith**...your heavenly Father knoweth that ye have need of all these things. But seek ye first the kingdom of God, and His righteousness; and all these things shall be added unto you."

Matthew 6:30, 32, 33

(Raging storm:) And the disciples came and woke Him, saying, "Master, Master, we are perishing!"...And He said to them, "[Why are you so fearful?] Where is your **faith** (your trust, your confidence in Me—in My veracity and My integrity)?"...and they marveled, saying to one another, "Who then is this, that He commands even wind and sea, and they obey Him?"

Luke 8:24, 25 AMP

(Storm on the sea:) And He saith unto them, "Why are ye fearful, O ye of **little faith**?"

Matthew 8:26a

And He arose, and rebuked the wind, and said unto the sea, "Peace, be still." And the wind ceased, and there was a great calm. And He said unto them, "Why are ye so fearful? how is it that ye have **no faith**?" *{We can speak peace to our circumstances, pain, a racing mind, or anything that is contrary to God.}*

Mark 4:39, 40

"And behold, a **spirit** seizes him and suddenly he cries out; it convulses him so that he foams at the mouth..." *{Note that the source of the convulsions is clearly stated as being a spirit.}* Jesus answered, "O [**faithless** ones]

unbelieving *and* **without trust** in God, a perverse (wayward, crooked and warped) generation!..." And even while he was coming, the **demon** threw him down, and [completely] convulsed him. But Jesus censured *and* severely rebuked the **unclean spirit** and healed the child and restored him to his father.

Luke 9:39, 41, 42 AMP

And Jesus answered, "O you **unbelieving** (warped, wayward, rebellious) and thoroughly perverse generation! How long am I to remain with you?"... And Jesus rebuked the demon, and it came out of him, and the boy was cured instantly. Then the disciples came to Jesus and asked privately, "Why could we not drive it out?" He said to them, "Because of the **littleness** of your **faith** [that is, your lack of firmly relying trust]. For truly I say to you, if you have **faith** [that is living] like a grain of mustard seed, you can say to this mountain, 'Move from here to yonder place,' and it will move; and nothing will be impossible to you."

Matthew 17:17-20 AMP

And He answered them, "O **unbelieving** generation [**without any faith**]! How long shall I [have to do] with you? How long am I to bear with you? Bring him to Me."

Mark 9:19 AMP

For God's [holy] wrath *and* indignation are revealed from heaven against all ungodliness and unrighteousness of men, who in their wickedness repress *and* hinder the Truth *and* **make it inoperative.** *{Lack of faith for the Truth of healing will make God's Word inoperative in your life.}*

Romans 1:18 AMP

(Jesus in His home town:) And He was **not** able to do even one work of power there, except that He laid His hands on a few sickly people [and] cured them. And He marveled

because of their unbelief (their lack of faith in Him).
{Where there was no faith, Jesus was unable to heal!}
Mark 6:5, 6a AMP

And they were offended in Him. But Jesus said unto them, "A prophet is not without honour, save in his own country, and in his own house." And He did not many mighty works there because of their unbelief.
Matthew 13:57, 58

Therefore they could not **believe**. For Isaiah has also said: "He *{Satan}* has blinded their eyes and hardened and benumbed their [callous, degenerated] hearts to keep them from seeing with their eyes and understanding with their hearts and minds and repenting and turning to Me to heal them." [Isaiah 6:9, 10]
John 12:40 AMP

But with whom was He grieved forty years? was it not with them that had sinned, whose carcases fell in the wilderness? And to whom sware He that they should not enter into His rest, but to them that believed not? So we see that they [the Israelites] could not enter in because of unbelief. *{Unbelief kept the Israelites from entering into the promise of God; unbelief will also keep us from experiencing the promises of God.}*
Hebrews 3:17-19

But wilt thou know, O vain man, that faith without works is dead?
James 2:20

Even so faith, if it hath not works, is dead, being alone.
James 2:17

For as the body without the spirit is dead, so faith without works is dead also.
James 2:26

Painful Blood Clots Healed

"One evening at church during a special worship service, my ankle started hurting and swelling up. I have dealt with blood clots for ten years, so I recognized the symptoms. Before praying for me, Nancy talked to me about taking authority over such things and not allowing them to manifest in my body. She encouraged me to expect to be healed. After she prayed for me, she had me move my ankle around and start walking on it. It definitely felt better. As I continued to worship, my ankle still felt a little odd with a small amount of pain left and some swelling. After about an hour, I was twisting my ankle around again when I heard a loud pop. I looked around to see if others had heard it. After that, I was able to dance around and worship the Lord with no difficulty.

"Now if my ankle begins to hurt, I take authority and say, 'You have been healed by the Name of Jesus, and no pain may enter in!' Then I twist my ankle around, and the pain goes away. I thank Jesus every morning when I get up and sing praises to Him."—Kim

Know therefore that the LORD thy God, He is God, the faithful God, which keepeth covenant and mercy with them that love Him and <u>keep</u> His commandments to a thousand generations.

Deuteronomy 7:9

Be strong and let your heart take courage, all you who wait for *and* hope for *and* expect the Lord!

Psalm 31:24 AMP

Be still *and* rest in the Lord; wait for Him *and* patiently lean yourself upon Him; fret not yourself...

Psalm 37:7 AMP

{We need to reach the point Job did:} I have esteemed *and* treasured the Words of His mouth more than my necessary food.

Job 23:12b AMP

"I assure you, most solemnly I tell you, if anyone steadfastly believes in Me, he will himself be able to do the things that I do; and he will do **even greater** things than these, because I go to the Father." *{And consider what Jesus was doing: teaching, preaching, healing and raising people from the dead!}*

John 14:12 AMP

Do not fret *or* have any anxiety about anything, but in every circumstance *and* in everything, by prayer and petition (definite requests), with thanksgiving, continue to make your wants known to God. And God's peace…which transcends all understanding shall garrison *and* mount guard over your hearts and minds in Christ Jesus.

Philippians 4:6, 7 AMP

"Be still, and <u>know</u> that I am God: <u>I will be exalted</u> among the heathen, I will be exalted in the earth." The LORD of hosts is with us; the God of Jacob is our Refuge. *{One way we can exalt Him among the heathen is through healing, but we must <u>know</u> our God and His promises.}*

Psalm 46:10, 11

AUTHORITY OVER EVIL

Taking Authority Over Sickness and Disease

"For I am the Lord, I change not."

How God anointed Jesus of Nazareth with the Holy Ghost and with power: Who went about doing good, and **healing all** that were oppressed of the devil; for God was with Him.

Acts 10:38

...and they brought Him **all** who were sick, those afflicted with various diseases and torments, those under the power of demons, and epileptics, and paralyzed people, and He healed them.

Matthew 4:24 AMP

When the even was come, they brought unto Him many that were possessed with devils: and He cast out the spirits with His Word, and healed **all** that were sick.

Matthew 8:16

And devils also came out of many, crying out, and saying, "Thou art Christ the Son of God." And He rebuking them suffered them not to speak: for they knew that He was Christ.

Luke 4:41

(Paralytic on stretcher:) ...and when Jesus saw their **faith**, He said to the paralyzed man, "Take courage, son; your sins are forgiven *and* the penalty remitted" "But in order that you may know that the Son of Man has authority on earth to forgive sins *and* remit the penalty," He then said to the paralyzed man, "Get up! Pick up your sleeping pad and go to your own house." When the crowds saw it, they were struck with fear *and* awe; and they recognized God *and* praised *and* thanked Him, Who had given such power *and* authority to men.

Matthew 9:2, 6, 8 AMP

And He preached in their synagogues throughout all Galilee, and cast out devils. *{This same authority was given to us.}*

Mark 1:39

For this purpose the Son of God was manifested, that He might **destroy** the works of the devil. *{The works of the devil are sickness, fear, death, frustration, lies, pain, disease, depression, and more. They have been destroyed that we might live free of them.}*

1 John 3:8b

"Behold, I give unto you power to tread on serpents and scorpions, and over **all** the power of the enemy: and **nothing** shall by **any means** hurt you." *{"Power" here also means "authority". Neither power nor authority amounts to anything, however, if it is not exercised.}*

Luke 10:19

And when He had called unto Him His twelve disciples, He gave them **power** against <u>unclean spirits</u>, to cast them out, and to heal **all** manner of sickness and **all** manner of disease.

Matthew 10:1

Then Jesus called together the Twelve [apostles] and gave them power and **authority** over **all** demons, and to cure diseases, And He sent them out to announce *and* preach the kingdom of God, and to bring healing.

Luke 9:1, 2 AMP

Demons Group Together

It is clear to see that sicknesses are of the devil. When I minister in villages, most the people coming for prayer will complain of the same issue. One village will suffer an inordinate number of toothaches; another village will suffer from a stronghold of stomach problems; another with eye problems. In one village, at least 16 people came forward with three things wrong with them. They each suffered from eye troubles (like cataracts), stomach problems and then a third ailment. All were totally healed. One person had eye, stomach, and throat problems, as well as a cyst, and he was healed of everything.

You made him *{man}* to have dominion over the works of Your hands; You have put **all** things under his feet. *{This includes Satan and his wiles!}*

Psalm 8:6 AMP

You have crowned him with glory and honor *and set him over the works of Your hands,* [Psalm 8:4-6.] For You have put **everything** in subjection under his feet. Now in

109

putting everything in subjection to man, He left **nothing** outside [of man's] control. But at present we do not yet see all things subjected to him [man].

Hebrews 2:7b, 8 AMP

"As Thou hast sent Me into the world, even so have I also sent them into the world."

John 17:18

Then said Jesus to them again, "Peace be unto you: as My Father hath sent Me, even so send I you."

John 20:21

And ye are complete in Him, which is the Head of all principality and power:

Colossians 2:10

[God] disarmed the principalities and powers that were ranged against us and made a bold display and public example of them, in triumphing over them in Him and in it [the cross].

Colossians 2:15 AMP

...that through death He might destroy him that had the power of death, that is, the devil; and deliver them who through fear of death were all their lifetime subject to bondage. *{We are no longer subject to bondage to the devil—his power has been destroyed!}*

Hebrews 2:14b, 15

Giving thanks unto the Father, Which hath made us meet to be partakers of the inheritance of the saints in Light: Who hath delivered us from the power of darkness, and hath translated us into the kingdom of His dear Son:

Colossians 1:12, 13

So be subject to God. Resist the devil [stand firm against him], and he will flee from you. *{We must be submitted to*

God and not to sickness! Then we are in a position to resist the devil, and he must flee.}

James 4:7 AMP

For God hath not given us the spirit of fear; but of power, and of love, and of a sound mind. *{The spirit of fear is from the enemy; it is not of God. For this reason, we can take authority over the spirit of fear.}*

2 Timothy 1:7

Migraine Headaches

"For years, I suffered from migraine headaches. My vision would be disrupted with a large, sparkling area so that I could not read or look at much. To try to avoid experiencing all of the symptoms, I would darken my room and try to get to bed quickly. After learning about our authority over sickness, I began exercising that authority and resisting the devil instead of simply accepting the pain and bracing myself for the worst. For many years now, when my vision is suddenly disrupted with the beginning of a migraine, I immediately take my stand of faith. I get the victory every time; the symptoms all leave within just a few minutes. Praise be to God! Many others have also been set free from all sorts of headaches."—Nancy Insley

They that see thee *{Satan}* shall narrowly look upon thee, and consider thee, saying, "Is this the man that made the earth to tremble, that did shake kingdoms; That made the world as a wilderness, and destroyed the cities thereof; that opened not the house of his prisoners?"

Isaiah 14:16, 17

Ye are of God, little children, and have overcome them *{evil spirits}*: because greater is He that is in you, than he that is in the world.

1 John 4:4

...as He is, so are we in this world.

1 John 4:17

For whatsoever is born of God overcometh the world: and this is the victory that overcometh the world, even our **faith**. Who is he that overcometh the world, but he that believeth that Jesus is the Son of God? *{Satan is the god of this world (2 Corinthians 4:4). Born of God, we can exercise **our faith** and overcome the world and its god.}*

1 John 5:4, 5

"In the world ye shall have tribulation: but be of good cheer; I have overcome the world." *{He has overcome evil and taken back authority over it.}*

John 16:33

"And I will give unto thee the keys of the kingdom of heaven: and whatsoever thou shalt bind on earth shall be bound in heaven: and whatsoever thou shalt loose on earth shall be loosed in heaven." *{We can bind the evil spirits. For example, we can bind the spirit of fear and release the spirit of love, of power and of a sound mind.}*

Matthew 16:19

"Verily I say unto you, 'Whatsoever ye shall bind on earth shall be bound in heaven: and whatsoever ye shall loose on earth shall be loosed in heaven.'"

Matthew 18:18

"When the strong man, fully armed, ...guards his own dwelling, his belongings are undisturbed... But when one stronger than he attacks him and conquers him, he robs him of his whole armor on which he had relied and divides up *and* distributes all his goods as plunder (spoil)."

Luke 11:21, 22 AMP

Be sober, be vigilant; because your adversary the devil, as a roaring lion, walketh about, seeking whom he may devour: Whom **resist** <u>stedfast in the faith</u>, knowing that the same afflictions are accomplished in your brethren that are in the world.

1 Peter 5:8, 9

Surely He shall deliver thee from the snare of the fowler, and from the noisome pestilence.

Psalm 91:3a

There shall no evil befall thee, neither shall any plague come nigh thy dwelling.

Psalm 91:10a

Thou shalt tread upon the lion and adder: the young lion and the dragon shalt thou trample under feet.

Psalm 91:13

[The people of Capernaum] were astonished at His doctrine: for **His Word was with power**. And in the synagogue there was a man, which had a spirit of an unclean devil... And Jesus rebuked him... And they were all amazed, and spake among themselves, saying, "What a **Word** is this! for with <u>authority</u> and <u>power</u> He commandeth the unclean spirits, and they come out." *{As His children, we share in that power!}*

Luke 4:32, 33, 35, 36

"In the Name of Jesus Christ of Nazareth rise up and walk."

Acts 3:6

"If we this day be examined of the good deed done to the impotent man, by what means he is made whole; be it known unto you all, and to all the people of Israel, that **by the Name** of Jesus Christ of Nazareth, Whom ye crucified, Whom God raised from the dead, even by Him doth this man stand here before you whole."

Acts 4:9, 10

An Evil Spirit Leaves and Lupus Is Healed

"I started having swelling and pain in my joints when I was 17 years old. About that same time, my fingers were turning blue and white, and I developed ulcers on the ends of my fingers due to the lack of blood flow. My symptoms were puzzling to doctors, but after a few bouts of pericarditis (inflammation and infection in the lining and fluid sac around my heart), I was diagnosed with Lupus and Raynaud's Phenomena at age 20. I continued to have joint pain, swelling and pericarditis until I was 29 years old.

"After that, the symptoms seemed to abate, and I was fairly healthy for 19 years. Then in 2001, I developed a kidney disease associated with Lupus. I was very frightened at the time and was told that I was seriously ill. I struggled with that disease for three years, taking lots of medication with nasty side effects.

"In July of 2004, I became reacquainted with Nancy. She shared some healing verses in the Bible with me and taught me how to have victory over illness. I was very excited to hear what she had to say and how others suffering with illnesses were being healed through the power of the Holy Spirit. As she began to pray, I felt a peace come over me. Although I did not always understand the language she was speaking, I kept saying, "I agree." I was overcome with what could only be the Holy Spirit and began to pray in a language I had

never known before.

"After a time, I sensed a blackness in my body. I felt very cold, and everything seemed dark. As we continued to pray, I felt intense pain in my feet and legs.  *I could see a black "thing" rising up through my legs and clinging to my thighs as if it did not want to leave. The pain rose higher. Suddenly I saw that "thing" (an evil spirit) leave me. As soon as that happened, I was exhausted and fell into a kind of deep, peaceful sleep on the couch. When I came to, I felt wonderful! Now, after nearly 4 years, I continue to feel great, and I claim the healing power of Jesus every day. I thank Him for His love and His provision for me."—Janet*

(Go and bring forth fruit:) "...that whatsoever ye shall ask of the Father **in My Name**, He may give it you..."

John 15:16

"Verily, verily, I say unto you, 'Whatsoever ye shall ask the Father **in My Name**, He will give it you... ask, and ye shall receive, that your joy may be full.'"

John 16:23, 24

And there was in their synagogue a man with an unclean spirit; and he cried out, Saying, "Let us alone; what have we to do with Thee, thou Jesus of Nazareth? Art Thou come to destroy us? I know Thee who Thou art, the Holy One of God." And Jesus rebuked him, saying, "Hold thy peace, and come out of him."

Mark 1:23-25

And He arose out of the synagogue, and entered Simon's house. And Simon's wife's mother was taken with a great fever; and they besought Him for her. And He stood over her, and <u>rebuked the fever</u>; and it left her: and immediately she arose and ministered unto them. *{The fever had to obey Jesus.}*

Luke 4:38, 39

"But [just] <u>speak a word</u>, and my servant boy **will be healed**. For I also am a man [daily] subject to authority, with soldiers under me. And I say to one, 'Go,' and he goes; and to another, 'Come,' and he comes; and to my bond servant, 'Do this,' and he does it." Now when Jesus heard this, He marveled at him, and He turned and said to the crowd that followed Him, "I tell you, not even in [all] Israel have I found such great faith [as this]." And when the messengers...returned to the house, they found the bond servant *who had been ill* quite well again.

Luke 7:7b-10 AMP

And Jesus answered, "O you unbelieving (warped, wayward, rebellious) and thoroughly perverse generation! How long am I to remain with you?"... And Jesus **rebuked the demon**, and it came out of him, and the boy was cured instantly. Then the disciples came to Jesus and asked privately, "Why could we not drive it out?" He said to them, "Because of the **littleness** of your **faith** [that is, your lack of firmly relying trust]. For truly I say to you, if you have **faith** [that is living] like a grain of mustard seed, you can <u>say</u> to this mountain, 'Move from here to yonder place,' and it will move; and nothing will be impossible to you."

Matthew 17:17-20 AMP

"And behold, a **spirit** seizes him and suddenly he cries out; it convulses him so that he foams at the mouth..." *{Note that the source of the convulsions is clearly stated as being a spirit.}* Jesus answered, "O [**faithless** ones] **unbelieving** *and* **without trust** in God, a perverse (wayward, crooked and warped) generation!..." And even while he was coming, the **demon** threw him down, and [completely] convulsed him. But Jesus censured *and* severely **rebuked the unclean spirit** and healed the child and restored him to his father.

Luke 9:39, 41, 42 AMP

Jesus said unto him, "If thou canst believe, all things are possible to him that believeth." And straightway the father of the child cried out, and said with tears, "Lord, I believe; help Thou mine unbelief." When Jesus saw that the people came running together, He **rebuked the foul spirit**, saying unto him, "Thou dumb and deaf spirit, I charge thee, come out of him, and enter no more into him." And the spirit cried, and rent him sore, and came out of him: and he was as one dead; insomuch that many said, "He is dead." But Jesus took him by the hand, and lifted him up; and he arose.

Mark 9:23-27

And Jesus answered them, "Truly I say to you, <u>if</u> you have **faith** (a firm relying trust) and **do not doubt**, you will not only do what has been done to the fig tree, but even if you <u>say</u> to this mountain, 'Be taken up and cast into the sea,' it will be done. And **whatever** you ask for in prayer, having faith *and* [really] believing, you will receive."

Matthew 21:21, 22 AMP

[He sends us forth:] to have authority *and* power to *heal the sick and to* **drive out demons**.

Mark 3:15 AMP

And He...gave them authority *and* power over the unclean spirits. And they drove out many unclean spirits and anointed with oil many who were sick and cured them.

Mark 6:7, 13 AMP

"And these signs shall follow <u>them that **believe**</u>; In My Name shall they cast out devils; they shall speak with new tongues; they shall take up serpents; and if they drink any deadly thing, it shall not hurt them; they shall lay hands on the sick, and they shall recover."

Mark 16:17, 18

(Gadarene man living in tombs:) But when he saw Jesus afar off, he ran and worshipped Him, and cried with a loud voice, and said, "What have I to do with Thee, Jesus, Thou Son of the most high God? I adjure Thee by God, that Thou torment me not." For He said unto him, "Come out of the man, thou **unclean spirit**."

Mark 5:6-8

Set Free From a Spiritual Attack

"I went to work as normal, and during the day I began getting stomach cramps. They continued to get worse and worse to the point that I was not even able to stand up as the pain was very intense.

"A good friend brought me home and called some other friends who prayed with me. They advised me to get to the emergency room as quickly as possible to find out what was wrong. My husband came home about that time and recognized that this was probably a spiritual attack of the enemy. He made a call to Nancy Insley, and we prayed together over the phone, taking authority over the demonic power. We agreed  *together that I was healed. I started to praise the Lord and to thank Him for healing me and taking away the pain. I was completely set free, and all the pain left me. This was almost two years ago, and I have not had any problem like that since."—Angie*

(Demon-possessed Gadarene:) They also which saw it told them by what means he that was possessed of the devils was healed. *[Jesus exercised authority over the evil spirits. Evil spirits cause sickness and insanity.]*

Luke 8:36

And when He was come to the other side into the country of the Gergesenes, there met Him two possessed with devils, coming out of the tombs, exceeding fierce, so that no man might pass by that way. And, behold, they cried out, saying, "What have we to do with Thee, Jesus, Thou Son of God? Art Thou come hither to torment us before the time?"
And there was a good way off from them an herd of many swine feeding. So the devils besought Him, saying, "If Thou cast us out, suffer us to go away into the herd of swine." And He said unto them, "Go." And when they were come out, they went into the herd of swine: and, behold, the whole herd of swine ran violently down a steep place into the sea, and perished in the waters.
And they that kept them fled, and went their ways into the city, and told every thing, and what was befallen to the possessed of the devils. *[Notice that the demons knew they were under the authority of Jesus and would need to obey.]*

Matthew 8:28-33

Now after this the Lord chose *and* appointed seventy others and sent them out ahead of Him, two by two, into every town and place where He Himself was about to come (visit). "And heal the sick in it and say to them, 'The kingdom of God has come close to you.'" The seventy returned with joy, saying, "Lord, even the demons are subject to us in Your Name!"

Luke 10:1, 9, 17 AMP

For if because of one man's trespass (lapse, offense) death reigned through that one, much more surely will those who

119

receive [God's] overflowing grace (unmerited favor) and the free gift of righteousness [putting them into right standing with Himself] <u>reign as kings in life</u> through the one Man Jesus Christ (the Messiah, the Anointed One). *{Satan, the god of this world, no longer has dominion over us; but instead, we, as children of God, have dominion and power over the devil.}*

Romans 5:17 AMP

Know ye not, that to whom ye yield yourselves servants to obey, his servants ye are to whom ye obey; whether of sin unto death, or of obedience unto righteousness? *{When we choose not to believe God's Word, we are believing the devil and not obeying God.}*

Romans 6:16

And He was casting out a devil, and it was dumb. And it came to pass, when the devil was gone out, the dumb spake; and the people wondered. *{Again we see that the unhealthy condition was caused by demonic oppression.}*

Luke 11:14

Bent Over at the Waist

One woman came to me fully bent over at the waist. Just like the woman in the Bible, she was unable to stand upright. She spent her days in pain and looking at the ground. How miserable! When I laid my hand on her, she immediately straightened up and started jumping around praising God, full of joy and thankfulness!

And there was a woman there who for eighteen years had had an infirmity caused by a **spirit** (a **demon of sickness**). She was bent completely forward and utterly unable to straighten herself up *or* to look upward. And when Jesus saw her, He called [her to Him] and said to her, "Woman, you are released from your infirmity!"

Luke 13:11, 12 AMP

"And ought not this woman, a daughter of Abraham, whom **Satan has kept bound** for eighteen years, be loosed from this bond on the Sabbath day?"

Luke 13:16 AMP

"And lead us not into temptation, but deliver us from evil: For Thine is the kingdom, and the power, and the glory, for ever. Amen."

Matthew 6:13

And what is the exceeding greatness of His power to us-ward who believe, according to the working of His mighty power, which He wrought in Christ when He raised Him from the dead, and set Him at His own right hand in the heavenly places, far above **all** principality, and power, and might, and dominion, and every name that is named, not only in this world, but also in that which is to come: and hath put **all** things under His feet, and gave Him to be the head over all things to the church *{As His children, we are given this same power and authority with all things under our feet.}*

Ephesians 1:19-22

For He [the Father] has put all things in subjection under His [Christ's] feet. But when it says, "All things are put in subjection [under Him]," it is evident that He [Himself] is excepted Who does the subjecting of all things to Him. *{God put sickness under Christ's feet and removed the authority of Satan over us. As Christ's Body, all things are now in subjection to us, as well.}*

1 Corinthians 15:27 AMP

He was listening to Paul as he talked, and [Paul] gazing intently at him and observing that <u>he</u> had faith to be healed, shouted at him, saying, "Stand erect on your feet!" And he leaped up and walked.

Acts 14:9, 10 AMP

And it came to pass, as we went to prayer, a certain damsel possessed with a spirit of divination met us, which brought her masters much gain by soothsaying: The same followed Paul and us, and cried, saying, "These men are the servants of the most high God, which shew unto us the way of salvation." And this did she many days. But Paul, being grieved, turned and said to the <u>spirit</u>, "I command thee in the Name of Jesus Christ to come out of her." And he came out the same hour *[the same instant]*.

Acts 16:16-18

The chief captain commanded him (Paul) to be brought into the castle, and bade that he should be examined by scourging; that he might know wherefore they cried so against him. And as they bound him with thongs, Paul said unto the centurion that stood by, "Is it lawful for you to scourge a man that is a Roman, and uncondemned?" When the centurion heard that, he went and told the chief captain, saying, "Take heed what thou doest: for this man is a Roman." Then the chief captain came, and said unto him, "Tell me, art thou a Roman?" He said, "Yea." And the chief captain answered, "With a great sum obtained I this freedom." And Paul said, "But I was free born." Then <u>straightway</u> they departed from him which should have examined him: and the chief captain also was afraid, after he knew that he was a Roman, and because he had bound him. *[When we understand <u>our</u> citizenship and speak out with authority against evil, the bondage (sickness, sin, fear) will also be loosed from us in this same manner.]*

Acts 22:24-29

122

And the people with one accord gave heed unto those things which Philip spake, hearing and seeing the miracles which he did. For **unclean spirits**, crying with loud voice, came out of many that were possessed with them: and many taken with palsies, and that were lame, were healed.

Acts 8:6, 7

"My Son Will Live and Not Die!"

"Our son, Andrew, was outside with his sister, Christa, who was talking on the phone. The phone's battery was running low, so Christa asked Andrew to run into the house to get the other phone. It had gotten dark outside, but the light was on inside. Looking to the side at the airplane in his hand, Andrew ran right through the heavy glass patio door. Actually, he only made it halfway, where he remained pinned in by huge glass shards. We heard the loud crash, but thought the large canner had slipped off the counter. Then I heard Andrew say, "Mom...help." I ran from the back room. We had just come home from shopping moments before. I stepped into the glass pieces barefoot and knelt down in them to try and break the glass away from Andrew so he could get out. I could see he was bleeding from his head where he had made contact with the door. He had a large open cut on his calf, one on his thigh, and a small one on his foot.

"The glass was so thick that I had to push with all my might, while Andrew waited patiently in his running stride, halfway inside and halfway outside the house. I was finally able to break away the jagged point from his left side. I asked him to move slightly in that direction so I could break out the other side. When he did that, I could

see that his whole back was split open! The slice was a foot long and at least an inch deep. It stretched across his backbone and wrapped around and down to his side. The cut was spread wide open. I called for my husband so that I could call 911. We got Andrew to the kitchen floor and waited for the paramedics to arrive. We were just learning about our authority in Christ. I immediately began taking that authority. I bound the spirit of fear and the spirit of death. Repeatedly, I declared that my son would live and not die and that he would have <u>no</u> pain and suffer no consequences from this injury.

"The wound on his back was so great, that the paramedics were quite taken by surprise. They quickly tore off his clothes and began placing large, sterile pads against his back. They were confident that he must have punctured his lungs and other organs. At the hospital, the doctors were fairly unconcerned at first glance. When I directed them to look at his back, they also started hustling. Being a holiday, surgeons, anesthesiologists and others were quickly called back to the hospital. In addition to the large slice on his back, other surgeons worked on the deep cut on his forehead and the severed tendon in his foot. Despite all these cuts and three hours of sewing and stapling him back together, he 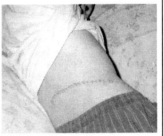 *experienced absolutely no pain! He was never given a single pain pill. Even during the days of recovery, he suffered no pain! And our son lives with no ill effects! Our God is mighty!"—Nancy Insley*

But thanks be to God, Who gives us the victory [making us conquerors] through our Lord Jesus Christ.

1 Corinthians 15:57 AMP

Now the Lord is the Spirit, and where the Spirit of the Lord is, there is **liberty** (emancipation from bondage, freedom). [Isa. 61:1, 2] *{When we bind the spirit of infirmity, fear, etc. through the Name of the Lord and have His Spirit in us, we **will** be made free!}*

2 Corinthians 3:17 AMP

He has sent Me to bind up *and* heal the brokenhearted, to proclaim **liberty** to the [physical and spiritual] captives and the opening of the prison *and* of the eyes to those who are **bound**.

Isaiah 61:1b AMP

For though we walk (live) in the flesh, we are not carrying on our warfare according to the flesh *and* using mere human weapons. For the weapons of our warfare are not physical [weapons of flesh and blood], but they are mighty before God for the overthrow *and* destruction of strongholds.

2 Corinthians 10:3, 4 AMP

Put on God's whole armor..., that you may be able successfully to stand up against [all] the strategies *and* the deceits of the devil. For we are not wrestling with flesh and blood [contending only with physical opponents], but against the despotisms, against the powers, against [the master spirits who are] the world rulers of this present darkness, against the spirit forces of wickedness in the heavenly (supernatural) sphere.

Ephesians 6:11, 12 AMP

Above all, taking the shield of faith, wherewith ye shall be able to <u>quench</u> **all** the fiery darts of the wicked. And take the helmet of salvation, and the sword of the Spirit, which is the <u>Word of God</u>:

Ephesians 6:16, 17

For once you were darkness, but now you are Light in the Lord; walk as children of Light...

Ephesians 5:8 AMP

And hath raised us up together, and made us sit together in heavenly places in Christ Jesus... *{We are seated with Christ. From that seat of power, we take authority over the enemy. Christ expects His Body to be free of sickness, disease and other bondages.}*

Ephesians 2:6

Set Free to Serve God

One woman in Madagascar was being attacked by a demonic power, which would cause her to temporarily lose her vision each time she tried to read her Bible in public. We broke the power of that demon, handed her a Bible and asked her to read some verses to us. With perfect vision, she was able to read them to us and then to the entire crowd at the crusade. She had been set free!

Through You shall we push down our enemies; through Your Name shall we tread them under who rise up against us. *{Through Christ, we push down the enemies of sickness, disease, fear and hopelessness.}*

Psalm 44:5 AMP

"No weapon that is formed against thee shall prosper..."

Isaiah 54:17

"Is not this the fast that I (God) have chosen? to loose the bands of wickedness, to undo the heavy burdens, and to let the oppressed go free, and that ye break every yoke?"

Isaiah 58:6

And it shall come to pass in that day, that his burden shall be taken away from off thy shoulder, and his yoke from off thy neck, and the yoke shall be <u>destroyed</u> because of the anointing.

Isaiah 10:27

"And I will rebuke the devourer for your sakes..."

Malachi 3:11

Then they cried to the Lord in their trouble, and He saved them out of their distresses. He brought them out of darkness and the shadow of death and <u>broke apart</u> the bonds that held them. *{This includes the bonds of sickness and disease.}*

Psalm 107:13, 14 AMP

Stand fast therefore in the <u>liberty</u> wherewith Christ hath made us free, and be not entangled again with the <u>yoke</u> of bondage.

Galatians 5:1

I have strength for **all** things in Christ Who empowers me [I am ready for anything and equal to anything through Him Who infuses inner strength into me...].

Philippians 4:13 AMP

And I heard a loud voice saying in heaven, "Now is come salvation *{health, deliverance, rescue, safety}*, and strength, and the kingdom of our God, and the power of His Christ: for the accuser of our brethren is cast down, which accused them before our God day and night. And they <u>overcame</u> him by the blood of the Lamb, and by the word of their testimony..."

Revelations 12:10, 11

GOD ANSWERS PRAYER

God's Promises to Answer Proper Prayers

For God shows no partiality [undue favor or unfairness; with Him one man is not different from another].

For the eyes of the Lord are upon the righteous..., and His ears are attentive to their prayer.

1 Peter 3:12a AMP

O LORD my God, I cried unto Thee and Thou hast healed me.

Psalm 30:2

"Do not be like them, for your Father knows what you need before you ask Him."

Matthew 6:8 AMP

"Ask, and it shall be given you; seek, and ye shall find; knock, and it shall be opened unto you: For **every one** that asketh receiveth; and he that seeketh findeth; and to him that knocketh it shall be opened."

Matthew 7:7, 8

Blurred, Tunnel Vision

"As long as I can remember, I disliked reading. When I looked at a page, I could see clearly in the center of my vision, but all around the edges, everything was blurred. After only a few paragraphs, the window of clarity would begin to shrink, while the blurry portion would increasingly grow. This caused me to squint more and more as I tried to keep a portion clear. An array of colors flashed around the edges. Reading for school was very strenuous, and I was continually plagued with headaches.

"One afternoon, at the age of 16, I was explaining this problem to Nancy. She offered to pray for my eyes. The following day, after reading in my history book, I suddenly realized that my vision had totally cleared. I was able to read with no problem, and I had no headache! That was nearly two years ago, and my vision remains clear. In fact, when I was thoroughly examined two months later for military school, the doctors found nothing wrong!"—Dustin

So I say to you, "Ask *and* keep on asking and it shall be given you; seek *and* keep on seeking and you shall find; knock *and* keep on knocking and the door shall be opened to you. For everyone who asks *and* keeps on asking receives; and he who seeks *and* keeps on seeking finds;

and to him who knocks *and* keeps on knocking, the door shall be opened."

Luke 11:9, 10 AMP

"If you then, evil as you are, know how to give good *and* advantageous gifts to your children, how much more will your Father Who is in heaven [perfect as He is] give good *and* advantageous things to those who keep on asking Him!"

Matthew 7:11 AMP

"If a son shall ask bread of any of you that is a father, will he give him a stone? or if he ask a fish, will he for a fish give him a serpent?" *{Our heavenly Father wants to give us good things.}*

Luke 11:11

We know that God does not listen to sinners; but if anyone is God-fearing *and* a worshiper of Him and does His will, He listens to him.

John 9:31 AMP

But I know, that even now, whatsoever thou wilt ask of God, God will give it thee.

John 11:22

"Again I say unto you, That if two of you shall agree on earth as touching any thing that they shall ask, it shall be done for them of My Father which is in heaven. For where two or three are gathered together in My Name, there am I in the midst of them." *{This would imply that wherever believers gather, prayers will be answered.}*

Matthew 18:19, 20

And the apostles said unto the Lord, "Increase our faith." And the Lord said, "If ye had **faith** as a grain of mustard seed, ye might <u>say</u> unto this sycamine tree, 'Be thou plucked up by the root, and be thou planted in the sea'; and it should **obey** you." *{Speak in faith to the problem. Your prayer will be answered.}*

Luke 17:5, 6

And Jesus, replying, said to them, "Have faith in God [constantly]. Truly I tell you, whoever says to this mountain, 'Be lifted up and thrown into the sea!' and does not doubt at all in his heart but believes that what he says will take place, it will be done for him. For this reason I am telling you, whatever you ask for in prayer, believe (trust and be confident) that it is granted to you, and you will [get it]."

Mark 11:22-24 AMP

And Jesus answered them, "Truly I say to you, <u>if</u> you have faith (a firm relying trust) and **do not doubt**, you will not only do what has been done to the fig tree, but even if you <u>say</u> to this mountain, 'Be taken up and cast into the sea,' it will be done. And **whatever** you ask for in prayer, having faith *and* [really] believing, you will receive."

Matthew 21:21, 22 AMP

"And **all** things, **whatsoever** ye shall ask in prayer, **believing**, ye shall receive."

Matthew 21:22

"And **whatsoever** ye shall ask in My Name, that will I do, that the Father may be glorified in the Son. If ye shall ask **any thing** in My Name, I will do it."

John 14:13, 14

"If ye abide in Me, and My Words abide in you, ye shall ask <u>what ye will</u>, and it **shall** be done unto you."

John 15:7

(Go and bring forth fruit:) "...that whatsoever ye shall ask of the Father in My Name, He may give it you..."

John 15:16

"Verily, verily, I say unto you, 'Whatsoever ye shall ask the Father in My Name, He will give it you... ask, and ye shall receive, that your joy may be full.'"

John 16:23, 24

He Who did not withhold or spare [even] His own Son but gave Him up for us all, will He not also with Him freely and graciously give us **all** [other] things?

Romans 8:32 AMP

...He generously bestows His riches upon **all** who call upon Him [in faith].

Romans 10:12 AMP

"My Wrist Compressed Like an Accordion"

"One day my husband and I were wrestling and pretending to fight. Just as I swung to punch him in the shoulder, he threw that shoulder forward. It felt like my wrist compressed like an accordion, making me think of the commercials that show cars being tested and driven straight into a wall. It hurt so badly that I could not move it at all. Not being able to afford to go to the doctor, I bought a splint from the store.

"When I went to church that night, Nancy prayed for my hand and wrist, and immediately, I was able to move it around. The pain had drastically diminished. By the end of the evening, all the pain was completely gone!"— Michelle

Do not fret *or* have any anxiety about anything, but in every circumstance *and* in everything, by prayer and petition (definite requests), with thanksgiving, continue to make your wants known to God. And God's peace...which transcends all understanding shall garrison *and* mount guard over your hearts and minds in Christ Jesus.

Philippians 4:6, 7 AMP

And my God will **liberally** supply (fill to the full) your **every** need according to His riches in glory in Christ Jesus.

Philippians 4:19 AMP

And the very God of peace sanctify you wholly; and I pray God your whole <u>spirit</u> and <u>soul</u> and <u>body</u> be preserved blameless unto the coming of our Lord Jesus Christ. <u>Faithful</u> is He that calleth you, Who also will do it.

1 Thessalonians 5:23, 24

But let endurance *and* steadfastness *and* patience have full play *and* do a thorough work, so that you may be [people] perfectly and fully developed [with no defects], <u>lacking in nothing</u>...Only it must be in faith that he asks with no wavering (no hesitating, no doubting). For truly, let not such a person imagine that he will receive anything [he asks for] from the Lord.

James 1:4, 6a, 7 AMP

(Bleeding woman:) For she said, "If I may touch but His clothes, I shall be whole." And He said unto her, "Daughter, thy **faith** hath made thee whole; go in peace, and be whole of thy plague."

Mark 5:28, 34

And this is the confidence that we have in Him, that, if we ask **any** thing according to His will, He heareth us: And if we know that He hear us, **whatsoever** we ask, we know that we have the petitions that we desired of Him.

1 John 5:14, 15

And we receive from Him whatever we ask, because we [watchfully] obey His orders... *and* [habitually] practice what is pleasing to Him. And this is His order...: that we should believe in (put our faith and trust in and adhere to and rely on) the Name of His Son Jesus Christ... *{We must believe God's Word is true. Jesus is the Word. It is not enough to know of Him—we must know Him, know what His Word says, and believe It.}*

1 John 3:22, 23 AMP

Do not, therefore, fling away your fearless confidence, for it carries a great *and* glorious compensation of reward. For you have need of steadfast patience *and* endurance, so that you may perform *and* **fully** accomplish the will of God, and thus receive *and* carry away [and enjoy to the full] what is promised. *{Do not give up; have patience!}*

Hebrews 10:35, 36 AMP

Heart Hurt So Badly

Many have been healed of heart problems. Some have said that they can feel the pain leave, and they feel the healing taking place.

One baby had a rapidly-beating, hard-pounding heart and a bad cough. As I held him, I could feel the wild pounding settle right down to normal.

One girl came to me in tears of pain, because her heart hurt her so badly. It would appear that she received a new heart from God, because she started dancing around very excited that the pain was gone.

Delight yourself also in the Lord, and He will give you the desires *and* secret petitions of your heart.

Psalm 37:4 AMP

...You do not have, because you do not ask. *[God is willing to answer our prayers.]*

James 4:2c AMP

Ye ask, and receive not, because ye ask amiss...

James 4:3

Say unto them, "As truly as I live," saith the LORD, "as ye have spoken in Mine ears, so will I do to you" *[Listen carefully to your words, for God is hearing them. Are they words of life or words of sickness and of death?]*

Numbers 14:28

Thou hast given him his heart's desire, and hast not withholden the request of his lips.

Psalm 21:2

God is not a man, that He should lie; neither the son of man, that He should repent: hath He said, and shall He not do it? or hath He spoken, and shall He not make it good?

Numbers 23:19

For He **spoke**, and it was done; He commanded, and it stood fast.

Psalm 33:9 AMP

Know therefore that the LORD thy God, He is God, the faithful God, which keepeth covenant and mercy with them that love Him and <u>keep</u> His commandments to a thousand generations.

Deuteronomy 7:9

Commit thy way unto the LORD; trust also in Him; and He shall bring it to pass.

Psalm 37:5

For this child I prayed; and the LORD hath given me my petition which I asked of Him: *{God desires to answer our prayers.}*

1 Samuel 1:27

Thou shalt make thy prayer unto Him, and He shall hear thee...

Job 22:27

With my voice I cry to the Lord, and He hears and answers me out of His holy hill...

Psalm 3:4 AMP

The Lord listens *and* heeds when I call to Him.

Psalm 4:3b AMP

I sought the LORD, and He heard me, and delivered me from **all** my fears.

Psalm 34:4

"...I will visit you, and keep My good promise to you... For I know the thoughts *and* plans that I have for you," says the Lord, "thoughts *and* plans for welfare *and* peace *{lit.: health, welfare, wholeness, prosperity, peace, rest and safety}* and <u>not</u> for evil, to give you hope in your final outcome. Then you will call upon Me, and you will come and pray to Me, and I will hear *and* heed you. Then you will see Me, inquire for *and* require Me [as a vital necessity] and find Me when you search for Me with all your heart."

Jeremiah 29:10-13 AMP

May the Lord fulfill **all** your petitions.

Psalm 20:5b AMP

137

The eyes of the Lord are toward the [uncompromisingly] righteous and His ears are open to their cry.

Psalm 34:15 AMP

When the *righteous* cry for help, the Lord hears, and delivers them out of **all** their distress *and* troubles.

Psalm 34:17 AMP

"And call on Me in the day of trouble; I will deliver you, and you shall honor *and* glorify Me."

Psalm 50:15 AMP

As for me, I will call upon God; and the LORD shall save me. *{The phrase "save me" means "to give me victory, deliver me, preserve me," and more.}*

Psalm 55:16

She Ran Home to Bring Her Husband Back

A woman was healed of great head pain at an outdoor meeting we held in the Philippines. She was so excited that she ran home to bring her husband back to get his lungs healed. She brought him into the prayer line, and he was instantly healed as well.

And the prayer [that is] of **faith** will save him who is sick, and the Lord will restore him; and if he has committed sins, he will be forgiven. Confess to one another therefore your faults (your slips, your false steps, your offenses, your sins) and pray [also] for one another, that you may be healed *and* restored... The earnest (heartfelt, continued) prayer of a righteous man makes tremendous power available [dynamic in its working].

James 5:15, 16 AMP

... seeing He giveth to all life, and breath, and **all** things;

Acts 17:25b

If I regard iniquity in my heart, the Lord will not hear me; but certainly God has heard me; He has given heed to the voice of my prayer. Blessed be God, Who has not rejected my prayer nor removed His mercy *and* loving-kindness from being [as it always is] with me.

Psalm 66:18-20 AMP

...and You are abundant in mercy *and* loving-kindness to **all** those who call upon You. Give ear, O Lord, to my prayer; and listen to the cry of my supplications. In the day of my trouble I will call on You, for You will answer me.

Psalm 86:5b-7 AMP

"He shall call upon Me, and I will answer him: I will be with him in trouble; I will deliver him, and honour him."

Psalm 91:15

Then they cry unto the LORD in their trouble, and He saveth them out of their distresses.

Psalm 107:19

Then they cry to the Lord in their trouble, and He brings them out of their distresses.

Psalm 107:28 AMP

Then they cried to the Lord in their trouble, and He saved them out of their distresses. He brought them out of darkness and the shadow of death and broke apart the bonds that held them. *{This includes the bonds of sickness and disease.}*

Psalm 107:13, 14 AMP

Hear my voice, O God, in my complaint; guard *and* preserve my life from the terror of the enemy. *{Our enemy now is the devil.}*

Psalm 64:1 AMP

I called upon the LORD in distress: the LORD answered me...

Psalm 118:5

He will fulfil the desire of them that fear Him: He also will hear their cry, and will save them. *{"Save" means "preserve, bring victory, deliver".}*

Psalm 145:19

He will surely be gracious to you at the sound of your cry; when He hears it, He **will answer** you.

Isaiah 30:19b AMP

Then you shall call, and the Lord **will answer**; you shall cry, and He will say, "Here I am."

Isaiah 58:9a AMP

"And it shall be that before they call I **will answer**; and while they are yet speaking I will hear."

Isaiah 65:24

"Then you will call upon Me, and you will come and pray to Me, and I will hear *and* heed you."

Jeremiah 29:12 AMP

"Call to Me and I will answer you and show you great and mighty things..."

Jeremiah 33:3 AMP

"At the <u>beginning</u> of thy supplications the commandment (to the angel Gabriel) came forth, and I am come to shew thee..." *{God answers immediately.}*

Daniel 9:23

Then said He unto me, "Fear not, Daniel: for from the <u>first</u> <u>day</u> that thou didst set thine heart to understand, and to chasten (humble) thyself before thy God, thy words were heard, and I am come for thy words."

Daniel 10:12

Goiters, Growths, Tumors Gone!

I have seen a number of tumors and growths disappear instantly. Amongst them were uterine cysts, tumors on various parts of the body and goiters. I have felt these external growths simply disappear under my hand.

A pastor's wife came forward full of faith for the removal of a painful cyst on her ovary, and she received healing. All of the pain was gone, and she had the assurance of healing in her heart. A few days later, she went to her doctor's appointment and the cyst could not be found!

After a lady received prayer for a goiter, she quickly reached up to feel for it, only to discover that it was no longer there. A younger girl had a goiter on both sides of her neck that totally disappeared.

One young girl had a spinal tumor. When the doctors did surgery to remove it, they found that it had completely vanished—nothing was there for them to remove!

Another person also testified that a tumor completely disappeared after a prayer cloth was laid on it.

...Thus saith the LORD, the God of David thy father, "I have heard thy prayer, I have seen thy tears: behold, I will heal thee..."

2 Kings 20:5

...and they will return to the Lord, and He will listen to their entreaties and **heal** them.

Isaiah 19:22 AMP

Heal me, O Lord, and I shall be healed; save me and I shall be saved, for You are my praise.

Jeremiah 17:14 AMP

"So shall My Word be that goeth forth out of My mouth: it shall not return unto Me void, but it shall accomplish that which I please, and it shall prosper in the thing whereto I sent it." *{Will not return "void" means will not return "without being effective". God's Word will not return to Him without being effective and accomplishing what He desired.}*

Isaiah 55:11

Then said the LORD unto me, "Thou hast well seen: for I will hasten My Word to perform it."

Jeremiah 1:12

No good thing will He withhold from those who walk uprightly.

Psalm 84:11b AMP

...let us hold fast our profession. For we have not an High Priest which cannot be touched with the feeling of our infirmities; but was in all points tempted like as we are, yet without sin. Let us therefore come boldly unto the throne of grace, that we may obtain mercy, and find grace to help in time of need.

Hebrews 4:14b-16

The thing a wicked man fears shall come upon him, but the desire of the [uncompromisingly] righteous shall be granted.

Proverbs 10:24 AMP

The sacrifice of the wicked is an abomination to the LORD: but the prayer of the upright is His <u>delight</u>.

Proverbs 15:8

Now unto Him that is able to do exceeding abundantly above **all** that we ask or think, according to the <u>power</u> that worketh in <u>us</u>...

Ephesians 3:20

THE IMPORTANCE OF OUR WORDS

Scriptures Clarifying How Important Our Words Are

For God shows no partiality [undue favor or unfairness; with Him one man is not different from another].

...and His Name is called The Word of God. And out of His mouth goeth a sharp sword...which sword proceeded out of His mouth *{Words pierce; they can pierce the darkness of evil or of themselves be evil. God's Word in our mouths is sharper than any two-edged sword.}*
Revelations 19:13, 15, 21

God is not a man, that He should lie; neither the son of man, that He should repent: hath He said, and shall He not do it? or hath He spoken, and shall He not make it good?
Numbers 23:19

By the **Word** of the Lord were the heavens made, and all their host by the breath of His mouth.

Psalm 33:6 AMP

For He **spoke**, and it was done; He commanded, and it stood fast.

Psalm 33:9 AMP

"...for the mouth of the LORD has spoken it." *{What the Lord speaks is of great importance and is **true**. For example, "By the stripes of Jesus, you <u>are</u> healed!"}*

Isaiah 40:5

"...for My mouth it hath commanded" (Isaiah 34:16). "...for the mouth of the LORD hath spoken it" (Isaiah 40:5). "...the Word is gone out of My mouth in righteousness" (Isaiah 45:23). "I have declared the former things from the beginning; and they went forth out of My mouth, and I shewed them; I did them suddenly, and they came to pass" (Isaiah 48:3). "...for the mouth of the LORD hath spoken it" (Isaiah 58:14). *{Again and again we see the power of the spoken word; it brings things into being which did not previously exist. There are also numerous verses telling how God has put His Words and His commandments into **our** mouths. We have the responsibility to be continually speaking God's Words of faith—not words of doubt, unbelief nor sickness.}*

Isaiah 34-58

...that He might make thee know that man doth not live by bread only, but by every <u>Word</u> that proceedeth out of the mouth of the LORD doth man **live**. *{In order to live the life God wants you to live, you must speak and obey His Word.}*

Deuteronomy 8:3

(When tempted, Jesus responded:) "It is written, 'Man shall not live by bread alone, but by every **Word** that proceedeth out of the mouth of God.'"

Matthew 4:4

Say unto them, "As truly as I live," saith the LORD, "as ye have spoken in Mine ears, so will I do to you" *{Are your words full of life, or are they full of sickness and of death?}*

Numbers 14:28

"Not that which goeth into the <u>mouth</u> defileth a man; but that which cometh out of the mouth, this defileth a man."

Matthew 15:11

And He said, "That which cometh out of the man, that <u>defileth</u> the man."

Mark 7:20

"Do not ye yet understand, that whatsoever entereth in at the <u>mouth</u> goeth into the belly... But those things which proceed out of the <u>mouth</u> come forth from the heart..."

Matthew 15:17, 18

"For by your <u>words</u> you will be justified and acquitted, and by your <u>words</u> you will be condemned and sentenced."

Matthew 12:37

Thou shalt also **decree** a thing, and it shall be established unto thee: and the light shall shine upon thy ways.

Job 22:28

And the tongue is a fire, a world of iniquity: so is the **tongue** among our members, that <u>it defileth the whole body</u>, and setteth on fire the <u>course of nature</u>; and it is set on fire of hell.

James 3:6

Likewise, look at the ships: though they are so great and are driven by rough winds, they are steered by a very small rudder wherever the impulse of the helmsman determines. Even so the **tongue** is a little member, and it can boast of great things. See how much wood *or* how great a forest a tiny spark can set ablaze!

James 3:4, 5 AMP

Out of the same mouth proceedeth blessing and cursing. My brethren, these things ought not so to be. *{We can bless ourselves and others with God's promises, or we can curse ourselves and others with the negative, doubting words of the devil.}*

James 3:10

they bless with their mouth, but they curse inwardly. *{People are often speaking faith with their mouths, but inwardly, their faith is not behind their words.}*

Psalm 62:4b

How forcible are words of straightforward speech!

Job 6:25a AMP

How long will ye vex my soul, and break me in pieces with **words**? *{Our words are powerful.}*

Job 19:2

Draw nigh to God, and He will draw nigh to you. Cleanse your hands, ye sinners; and purify your hearts *{thoughts, feelings}*, ye double minded. *{We cannot speak God's Word and focus on the problem without being double-minded.}*

James 4:8

He said to them, "Because of the littleness of your **faith** [that is, your lack of firmly relying trust]. For truly I say to you, if you have **faith** [that is living] like a grain of mustard seed, you can **say** to this mountain, 'Move from here to yonder place.' and it will move; and nothing will be impossible to you." *{Do not use your mouth to confirm the negative circumstances but to move the mountains.}*

Matthew 17:20

And the apostles said unto the Lord, "Increase our faith." And the Lord said, "If ye had **faith** as a grain of mustard seed, ye might **say** unto this sycamine tree, 'Be thou plucked up by the root, and be thou planted in the sea'; and it should obey you." *{We must increase our own faith by hearing the Word and speaking it out.}*

Luke 17:5, 6

And Jesus answered them, "Truly I say to you, <u>if</u> you have faith (a firm relying trust) and **do not doubt**, you will not only do what has been done to the fig tree, but even if you **say** to this mountain, 'Be taken up and cast into the sea,' it will be done. And **whatever** you ask for in prayer, having faith *and* [really] believing, you will receive."

Matthew 21:21, 22 AMP

Jesus answered and said unto them, "Verily I say unto you, <u>if</u> ye have **faith**, and <u>doubt not</u>, ye shall not only do this which is done to the fig tree, but also if ye shall **say** unto this mountain, 'Be thou removed, and be thou cast into the sea;' it shall be done."

Matthew 21:21

Splitting Wedge Falls on Foot—No Injury!

"Mid-October, 2007, after a tiring day of trimming trees, splitting firewood and moving bales of hay until around 10 p.m., Mike and I began to put our tools away. I was carrying three five-pound splitting wedges with one arm when one dropped and hit the top, bony part of my foot, causing a searing pain. I am no stranger to injuries, as I

have received many while working around our farm. I believe that I had possibly broken a bone or two. The best I might have hoped for was a bad bruise to the top of my foot.

"My first reaction was, 'Oh, no!' Then I remembered how Nancy had told of falling and badly hurting her ankle. She had rebuked the injury and any damage to her ankle and was able to reject all limitations that such an injury would normally have brought. At that moment, the Holy Spirit took over my mouth, and I hollered, 'Hallelujah! The Lamb of God, the Prince of Peace, the Almighty One, my Lord and Savior, thank You for providing for my healing!' Words of praise were effortlessly pouring out my mouth. As I walked, the place of pain became a warm area the size of a silver dollar on the top of my foot. As I continued to praise the Lord, the warmth left, and absolutely no pain remained. Inside the house, when I removed my sock and shoe to check the damage, there was no sign of an injury, nor was there any bruise or discomfort the next day!

"I had attended three of Nancy's classes before this incident. I believe that I was so convinced of God's power to overcome Satan's attacks, that it seemed easy for me to change my words from honoring Satan's kingdom (as had been my habit) to honoring God's Kingdom. I focused on Him instead of the accident.

"Nancy had told us to disregard negative circumstances and to reject the devil's work and, instead, to rejoice in the Lord. It works! God wants us to be overcomers, not victims of the enemy's attacks."—Judy

And Jesus, replying, said to them, "Have faith in God [constantly]. Truly I tell you, whoever **says** to this mountain, 'Be lifted up and thrown into the sea!' and does not doubt at all in his heart but believes that what he **says** will take place, it will be done for him. For this reason I am telling you, whatever you ask for in prayer, believe (trust and be confident) that it is granted to you, and you will [get it]."

Mark 11:22-24

And He said, "So is the kingdom of God, as if a man should cast seed into the ground; ...and the seed should spring and grow up..." *{God's Seed is His Word. The words we speak are the seeds we plant. Cast good, godly seed onto the ground of your spirit.}*

Mark 4:26, 27

A man shall be satisfied with good by the fruit of his mouth...

Proverbs 12:14

A man shall eat good by the fruit of his mouth...

Proverbs 13:2

"A good man out of the good treasure of his heart bringeth forth that which is good; and an evil man out of the evil treasure of his heart bringeth forth that which is evil: for of the abundance of the heart his mouth speaketh." *{Is the abundance of your heart speaking faith and healing or doubt and sickness?}*

Luke 6:45

"...for out of the abundance of the heart the mouth speaketh."

Matthew 12:34

So then faith cometh by hearing, and hearing by the Word of God. *{The "Word of God" here is His spoken, "rhema"*

151

*Word. We, too, should **speak** His Word in order to build up our faith.}*

Romans 10:17

That in every thing ye are enriched by Him, in **all** utterance, and in all knowledge.

1 Corinthians 1:5

Now we have received, not the spirit of the world, but the Spirit which is of God; that we might know the things that are freely given to us of God *{like healing}*. Which things also we speak, not in the words which man's wisdom teacheth, but which the Holy Ghost teacheth; comparing spiritual things with spiritual. *{Healing is spiritual. God says in Zechariah 4:6 that it is "not by might, nor by power, but by My Spirit."}*

1 Corinthians 2:12, 13

For with the heart a person believes (adheres to, trusts in, and relies on Christ) and so is justified (declared righteous, acceptable to God), and with the <u>mouth he confesses</u> (declares openly and speaks out freely his faith) *and* confirms [his] salvation.

Romans 10:10 AMP

That if thou shalt <u>confess with thy mouth</u> the Lord Jesus, and shalt **believe** in thine heart...

Romans 10:9

Yet we have the same spirit of faith as he had who wrote, "I have believed, and therefore have I spoken." We too believe, and therefore we **speak**. *{Speaking God's Word is how we express our faith and spread His Word.}*

2 Corinthians 4:13 AMP

But we commend ourselves in every way as [true] servants of God:...by [speaking] the Word of Truth, in the power of God, with the weapons of righteousness for the right hand [to attack] and for the left hand [to defend]. *(You now know God's Truth about healing. Your weapon against the devil is <u>claiming</u> God's Word.)*

2 Corinthians 6:4, 7 AMP

Be not deceived; God is not mocked: for whatsoever a man soweth, that shall he also reap. *(Don't sow sickness with your words and actions; sow health.)*

Galatians 6:7

Neither murmur ye, as some of them also murmured, and were destroyed of the destroyer. *(See John 10:10.)*

1 Corinthians 10:10

Let no corrupt communication proceed out of your mouth, but that which is good to the use of edifying, that it may minister grace unto the hearers. *(Choose words of health which glorify God.)*

Ephesians 4:29

...idle talk leads only to poverty.

Proverbs 14:23 AMP

A fool's mouth is his destruction, and his lips are the snare of his soul.

Proverbs 18:7

Giving the Enemy Permission to Wound

"I was always saying, 'If it's going to happen, it will happen to me!' I also regularly called myself a 'klutz'. I was setting myself up for being accident prone, but I did not know it. I was giving the enemy plenty of permission to make 'accidents' happen on a regular basis: I was the only one who got thrown from the raft going down the Deschutes River. I was the one that tripped over nothing

going up the stairs. In getting off the chair lift to ski, I <u>fell</u> off instead. The dog would cause me to fall over, or he would knock me over. I slipped on black ice so many times, I lost count.

"The constant accidents often sent me to the chiropractor's office. I was so frustrated with constantly going there that I asked Nancy how I could stay away. Her answer was simple. She said, 'Listen to yourself. Listen to what comes out of your mouth.' Wow, was she right!

"I went home, spent time with God repenting for my negative expectations and determined to change. That very night, I went to a friend's Bible study. They have a 100-pound dog that knows me, but for absolutely no reason, he ran at me. I was knocked back against the wall. I was unhurt, but the dog was immediately put outside. I quickly recognized that the enemy was trying to instill doubt in me, making me believe that God had not 'healed' me from the constant accidents. In Jesus' Name, I rebuked the enemy. Ever since then, I have been 'accident free', and that was two years ago.

"I thank God for this wonderful change. Of course, I regularly tell others to watch what comes out of their mouths. When we pay attention to our words, it is amazing how it affects our lives and the lives of others. I still need to watch my own mouth. I pray the verse Psalm 141:3 – 'Set a guard, O Lord, over my mouth; Keep watch over the door of my lips' (NKJV)."—Rose

For Jerusalem is ruined, and Judah is fallen: because their **tongue** and their doings are against the LORD...

Isaiah 3:8

The wicked is [dangerously] snared by the transgression of his lips, but the [uncompromisingly] righteous shall come out of trouble.

Proverbs 12:13 AMP

The foolishness of man subverts his way [ruins his affairs]; then his heart is resentful *and* frets against the Lord. *{It is foolish to speak what does not agree with the Word of the Lord. People speak sickness, disease and negative doctors' reports and then become resentful against God for not healing them—but they have subverted their own way!}*

Proverbs 19:3 AMP

Thou art snared with the words of thy mouth, thou art taken with the words of thy mouth. *{Speak God's Words about healing that you might not be snared.}*

Proverbs 6:2

By the blessing of the upright the city is exalted: but it is overthrown by the mouth of the wicked. *{We can quickly undo good with the words of our mouth.}*

Proverbs 11:11

The words of a wise man's mouth are gracious; but the lips of a fool will swallow up himself.

Ecclesiastes 10:12

Seest thou a man that is hasty in his words? there is more hope of a fool than of him. *{Do not be hasty to speak about a sickness. Consider first what God's Word says, and choose to agree with Him.}*

Proverbs 29:20

O Timothy, guard *and* keep the deposit entrusted [to you]! Turn away from the irreverent babble *and* godless chatter, with the vain *and* empty *and* worldly phrases, and the subtleties *and* the contradictions in what is falsely called knowledge *and* spiritual illumination. *{"I'm dying for* some chocolate!" "It scared me to <u>death</u>..." "I could have <u>died</u> when..." "I <u>always</u> forget..." "I <u>always</u> get <u>sick</u> when..." "It makes me <u>sick</u> to hear that..."}

1 Timothy 6:20 AMP

Malaria Healed

One man was gravely ill with malaria; he was not given long to live. We visited him in his home, and I shared some Scriptures with him. We also anointed a cloth to leave with him. The following day, we received the news that the man was up out of bed and feeling fine!

In another country, one girl was lying on the ground very ill with malaria <u>and</u> HIV. After I explained salvation to her and laid hands on her for healing, there was an immediate change in her countenance. Her headache and stomachache were gone, and she said that she felt really good. The girls who were with me exclaimed, "She looked <u>really</u> ill before, but now she even <u>looks</u> like she feels good!"

I have seen several others with malaria, whose symptoms disappeared immediately. One woman was healed in the marketplace and began testifying to others.

Another girl had collapsed in pain on the playground. She had a horrible headache with visible swelling in her head. As soon as I laid hands on her, we could see the swelling disappear, and she stopped cringing in pain.

The same has been true for HIV/AIDS victims. After prayer, they exclaim that the pain has left and that they feel wonderful.

Finally, brethren, whatsoever things are true, whatsoever things are honest, whatsoever things are just, whatsoever things are pure, whatsoever things are lovely, whatsoever things are of good report; if there be any virtue, and if there be any praise, think on these things. *{Do not think on illness. What you think on is key to what you will receive.}*

Philippians 4:8

Fight the good fight of faith, lay hold on eternal life, whereunto thou art also called, and hast professed a good profession before many witnesses. *{A good profession will agree with the Word of God.}*

1 Timothy 6:12

For the Word that God speaks is alive and full of **power** [making it active, operative, energizing, and effective]... *{Made in His image, your words also carry power. Are your words agreeing with God or with the work of the devil?}*

Hebrews 4:12a AMP

...upholding all things by the **word** of His power...

Hebrews 1:3

"Is not My Word like as a fire?" saith the LORD; "and like a hammer that breaketh the rock in pieces?" *{God's Word is so very powerful.}*

Jeremiah 23:29

"So shall My Word be that goeth forth out of My mouth: it shall not return unto Me void, but it shall accomplish that which I please, and it shall prosper in the thing whereto I sent it." *{Will not return "void" means will not return "without being effective". God's Word will not return to Him without being effective and accomplishing what He desired. What a wonderful promise!}*

Isaiah 55:11

(As it is written, "I have made thee a father of many nations,") before Him whom he believed, even God, who quickeneth the dead, and **calleth those things which be not as though they were**. *{Another valid translation is: "calls things that are not so that they are."}*

Romans 4:17

Let us hold fast the <u>profession</u> of our faith <u>without wavering</u>; (for He is **faithful** that promised).

Hebrews 10:23

...let us hold fast our profession. *{Watch what you are speaking!}*

Hebrews 4:14b

For let him who wants to enjoy life and see good days...keep his **tongue** free from evil and his **lips** from guile (treachery, deceit). *{Your words are important to your welfare!}*

1 Peter 3:10 AMP

For the sin of their mouth and the words of their lips let them even be taken in their pride...

Psalm 59:12

They set their mouth **against** the heavens... *{This is what we do when we speak the evil report.}*

Psalm 73:9

By Him therefore let us offer the sacrifice of praise to God continually, that is, the fruit of our lips giving thanks to His Name. *{Listen to the fruit of your lips.}*

Hebrews 13:15

Through faith we understand that the worlds were framed by the **Word** of God, so that things which are seen were not made of things which do appear. *{"Which do appear"* *means "which are visible". God's Word has the power to create. Our words of faith carry that same power.}*

Hebrews 11:3

Itching Scale

"In 2008, I was attacked with an itching scale over most of my body. The doctors did not know what it was. They thought that it might be caused by a food allergy, so they gave me medication, which did not help. Nancy prayed for me, and the itching stopped, but the scales were still there. After a while, the itching returned.

"As I was praying in the Spirit, the Word kept coming to me 'Wherefore take unto you the whole armour of God, that ye may be able to withstand in the evil day, and having done all, to stand' (Ephesians 6:13); for the devil comes to kill, to steal and to destroy. I knew that it was up to me to keep my healing. I began confessing that I had the victory and that I was free from all  curses. I declared that every cell and tissue operated in the perfection of God. My skin turned soft and smooth, and I was free of itching. With no change in my diet, I have remained healed."—Jody

I will bless the LORD at all times: His praise shall continually be in my mouth. *{It is better to have words of praise in your mouth than words of sickness.}*

Psalm 34:1b

For they willfully overlook *and* forget this [fact], that the heavens [came into] existence long ago by the <u>Word</u> of God... *{God's Word creates.}*

2 Peter 3:5a AMP

Death and life are in the power of the tongue, and they who indulge in it shall eat the fruit of it [for death or life].

Proverbs 18:21 AMP

A man's [moral] self shall be filled with the fruit of his mouth; and with the consequence of his words he must be satisfied [whether good or evil].

Proverbs 18:20 AMP

But we will certainly do whatsoever thing goeth forth out of our own mouth... *{This was spoken in rebellion. Are you speaking God's Words or your own?}*

Jeremiah 44:17

There are those who speak rashly, like the piercing of a sword, but the tongue of the wise brings **healing**.

Proverbs 12:18 AMP

Pleasant words are as a honeycomb, sweet to the mind and **healing** to the body.

Proverbs 16:24 AMP

When I kept silence [before I confessed], my bones wasted away through my groaning all the day long. *{Unconfessed sin can make us ill. Our words are important.}*

Psalm 32:3 AMP

The tongue of the just is as choice silver...

Proverbs 10:20

...the lips of the wise shall preserve them.

Proverbs 14:3

In the lips of him that hath understanding wisdom is found...

Proverbs 10:13

The mouth of the righteous speaketh wisdom... *{It is not wisdom to speak against God's Word by speaking sickness and evil reports from the doctors.}*

Psalm 37:30

The heart of the wise teacheth his mouth, and addeth learning to his lips.

Proverbs 16:23

Set a watch, O LORD, before my mouth; keep the door of my lips.

Psalm 141:3

Aching Shoulder

The pastor from the first church where I preached in Madagascar had a shoulder which had been hurting him so badly that he couldn't lift his arm. He had been ready to go to the doctor, but he let me pray for him that first day. He was totally healed and began excitedly to swing his arm around in circles. He followed us to every meeting for the next three weeks, testifying to his healing and excitedly explaining to each congregation what he was learning: he didn't need to accept everything the devil was offering, he could resist sickness, and he could exercise faith for healing. He had found the Truth, and it had set him free! Praise the Lord!

Therefore shall they eat of the fruit of their own way *{conversation}*, and be filled with their own devices *{purposes, counsel}*.

Proverbs 1:31

Who have said, "With our **tongue** will we prevail; <u>our **lips** are our own</u>: who is lord over us?" *{What is your tongue speaking?}*

Psalm 12:4

...I will take heed to my ways, that I sin not with my tongue: I will keep my mouth with a bridle...

Psalm 39:1

...I have purposed that my **mouth** shall not transgress. *{Agree with what God has said in His Word.}*

Psalm 17:3 AMP

Let them now that fear the LORD **say**, that His mercy endureth forever. *{We need to <u>say</u> what God's Word promises, no matter what the circumstances are. If, instead, we speak sickness, then we are not believing for healing. (See Matthew 12:34.)}*

Psalm 118:4

I believed, therefore have I spoken. *{Speak God's Word about healing.}*

Psalm 116:10a

Let the redeemed of the LORD say so, whom He hath redeemed from the hand of the enemy; *{That's us! We must confess who we are in Christ.}*

Psalm 107:2

"This book of the law <u>shall not depart out of thy **mouth**</u>; but thou shalt meditate therein day and night, that thou mayest observe to do according to all that is written therein: for then thou shalt make thy way prosperous, and then thou shalt have good success."

Joshua 1:8

And they that know Thy Name will put their trust in Thee: for Thou, LORD, hast not forsaken them that seek Thee.

Psalm 9:10

The Words of the LORD are pure Words: as silver tried in a furnace of earth, purified seven times.

Psalm 12:6

Every Word of God is pure: He is a shield unto them that put their trust in Him.

Proverbs 30:5

Concerning the works of men, by the Word of Your lips I have avoided the ways of the violent (the paths of the destroyer).

Psalm 17:4 AMP

Let the **words** of my mouth, and the meditation of my heart, be acceptable in Thy sight, O LORD, my Strength, and my Redeemer.

Psalm 19:14

My mouth shall speak wisdom; and the meditation of my heart shall be understanding.

Psalm 49:3

And Caleb stilled the people before Moses, and said, "Let us go up at once, and possess it *{the Promised Land}*; for we are well able to overcome it." But the men that went up with him said, "We be not able to go up against the people; for they are stronger than we." And they brought up an evil report of the land which they had searched unto the children of Israel, saying, "The land, through which we have gone to search it, is a land that eateth up the inhabitants thereof; and all the people that we saw in it are men of a great stature. And there we saw the giants, the sons of Anak, which come of the giants: and we were <u>in our own sight as grasshoppers</u>, and so we were in their sight." *{Are you speaking the "evil report"? Are you seeing yourself as victorious through the promises of God, or are you accepting defeat, seeing yourself as a "grasshopper" because of an evil report from a doctor? Note Caleb's response: "We are well able to overcome it."}*

Numbers 13:30-33

Wherefore laying aside all malice, and all guile, and hypocrisies, and envies, and all <u>evil speakings</u>, As newborn babes, desire the sincere milk of the Word, that ye may grow thereby: *{Don't agree with the enemy nor circumstances; agree with God.}*

1 Peter 2:1, 2

Behold, the LORD thy God hath set the land before thee: go up and possess it, as the LORD God of thy fathers hath said unto thee; "Fear not, neither be discouraged." *{The Promised Land is like the promises of God to us now: if we do not fear but speak what He has spoken, we will "go up and possess them".}*

Deuteronomy 1:21

Deaf and Dumb Speak, "Hallelujah!"

I have prayed for several folks who have been deaf or even deaf and dumb. What a tremendous blessing it is to hear the first words out of their mouths. Typically it is, "Hallelujah!" This lovely praise has even come from the mouths of those who have never spoken before! This clearly shows that the spirit man is alive unto God and is a separate entity from the natural man.

One young girl in the Philippines had been deaf in one ear. She was so excited when that ear opened right up and she could hear clearly.

Another girl in the Philippines, who was deaf in one ear, was having to turn her good ear to me every time I spoke with her. When I asked if she wanted prayer for the deaf ear, she shrugged her shoulders but accepted. After praying for her, she continued talking, completely ignoring the prayer. I stopped her and asked if she could now hear. To her amazement, she could hear perfectly!

One day in the grocery store in Oregon, I noticed the teller turning her head that same way in order to hear me. I asked if she was having trouble with her ear. She said that it was going deaf, but she could not go to the doctor until her medical insurance coverage began. She was quite taken aback when I asked if she would receive prayer. She said that she would, so we stopped and prayed. Immediately, she could hear perfectly in both ears. After she was off work, she called all of her family members to tell them the good news!

he who guards his way preserves his life. *{This can also read: He who guards his conversation preserves his life.}*

Proverbs 16:17b AMP

Keep thy tongue from evil, and thy lips from speaking guile.

Psalm 34:13

The words of his mouth are wrong... *{The words of our mouth are wrong when they are speaking sickness and defeat.}*

Psalm 36:3 AMP

In a multitude of words transgression is not lacking, but he who restrains his lips is prudent. *{Watch what words you will allow to come out of your mouth.}*
                                              Proverbs 10:19 AMP

...moving his lips he bringeth evil to pass.
                                              Proverbs 16:30

The words of the wicked are to lie in wait for blood: but the **mouth** of the upright shall <u>deliver</u> them.
                                              Proverbs 12:6

If you have done foolishly in exalting yourself, or if you have <u>thought evil</u>, lay your hand upon your mouth. *{Focusing on the doctor's report instead of God's Word is evil in His sight. Speak His Word, or say nothing at all.}*
                                              Proverbs 30:32 AMP

He who guards his mouth keeps his **life**, but he who opens wide his lips comes to ruin.
                                              Proverbs 13:3 AMP

He who guards his mouth and his tongue keeps himself from troubles *{adversity, distress}*.
                                              Proverbs 21:23 AMP

Wise men store up knowledge [in mind and heart], but the mouth of the foolish is a present destruction.
                                              Proverbs 10:14 AMP

...and their tongue a sharp sword.
                                              Psalm 57:4

Who whet their tongue like a sword... *{Our words...}*
                                              Psalm 64:3

Behold, they belch out with their mouth: swords are in their lips: "for who," say they, "doth hear?" *{The spiritual realm does!}*

Psalm 59:7

Get wisdom, get understanding: forget it not; neither decline from the words of my mouth. Forsake her *{wisdom}* not, and she shall preserve thee: love her, and she shall keep thee. Hear, O my son, and receive my sayings; and the years of thy life shall be many. *{Wise words in your mouth will preserve you and bring you long life.}*

Proverbs 4:5, 6, 10

Then said He unto me, "Fear not, Daniel: for from the <u>first day</u> that thou didst set thine heart to understand, and to chasten (humble) thyself before thy God, thy words were heard, and I am come for thy words."

Daniel 10:12

Be not rash with thy mouth, and let not thine heart be hasty to utter any thing before God...

Ecclesiastes 5:2

Do not allow your mouth to cause your body to sin...

Ecclesiastes 5:6 AMP

Hear, for I will speak excellent *and* princely things; and the opening of my lips shall be for <u>right</u> things. For my mouth shall utter truth...All the words of my mouth are righteous (upright and in right standing with God); there is nothing contrary to truth or crooked in them.

Proverbs 8:6-8 AMP

The mouth of a righteous man is a well of **life**...

Proverbs 10:11

Healed of Cancer

"In January of 2004, I had my annual female exam. A few days later, I was called into the doctor's office because the pap smear had tested positive for cancer. I was sent to have several biopsies taken. The doctors were concerned that, at the age of 21, I would need a full hysterectomy due to the amount of cancer and the fact that it was spreading so rapidly. I was frightened and called my mom (Nancy Insley). Understanding the importance of words and that faith increases by hearing, she counseled me not to say a word to anyone. She  *prayed with me over the phone. She was convinced that God's power was greater than the cancer and that all was well.*

"A few days later, the biopsies were repeated. When I was called into the office, the doctor was confused. He said, 'I don't understand it, but the tests are negative. This should not be! We need to do a such-and-such test.' I answered, 'They already did.' The doctor questioned, 'They did? What were the results?' 'Negative.'

"The doctor could not comprehend what had happened. Astounded, he responded, 'They were?? I don't understand this! I know there was cancer; I could see it in the tests!'

"Whose report will you believe? I will believe the report of the Lord!"—Christa

A man hath joy by the answer of his mouth... *{Is your mouth bringing you joy or depression and helplessness?}*
Proverbs 15:23

A gentle tongue [with its <u>healing</u> power] is a tree of life, but willful <u>contrariness</u> in it breaks down the spirit.
Proverbs 15:4 AMP

The chief captain commanded him (Paul) to be brought into the castle, and bade that he should be examined by scourging; that he might know wherefore they cried so against him. And as they bound him with thongs, Paul said unto the centurion that stood by, "Is it lawful for you to scourge a man that is a Roman, and uncondemned?" When the centurion heard that, he went and told the chief captain, saying, "Take heed what thou doest: for this man is a Roman." Then the chief captain came, and said unto him, "Tell me, art thou a Roman?" He said, "Yea." And the chief captain answered, "With a great sum obtained I this freedom." And Paul said, "But I was free born." Then <u>straightway</u> they departed from him which should have examined him: and the chief captain also was afraid, after he knew that he was a Roman, and because he had bound him. *{When we understand <u>our</u> citizenship and speak out with authority, the bondage (sickness, sin, fear) will also be loosed in this same manner.}*
Acts 22:24-29

(As it is written, "I have made thee a father of many nations,") before Him whom he believed, even God, who quickeneth the dead, and <u>calleth those things which be not as though they were</u>. *{God acted in faith when He spoke out things that did not yet exist. When <u>we</u> do that, people say we are lying, but it is truly acting in faith—it is trusting in God. God <u>cannot</u> lie, and He is our example. Another translation of the phrase "calleth those things which be not as though they were" is "calls those things which are not <u>so that</u> they are". Note, also, that God said,*

169

"I have made thee a father of many nations." Abram did
not have a son for many years thereafter, but God spoke as
if it were an accomplished fact—He spoke what was not,
as though it were. *(Please read the rest of this passage
through verse 22 under "Faith Versus Doubt".)}*

Romans 4:17

(Bleeding woman:) For she kept **saying,** "If I only touch
His garments, I shall be restored to health." *{She was
speaking her faith, not her current condition.}*

Mark 5:28

(Bleeding woman:) And when the woman saw that she
was not hid, she came trembling, and falling down before
Him, she declared unto Him before all the people for what
cause she had touched Him, and how she was healed
immediately. *{She was declaring and confirming her
healing.}*

Luke 8:47

"But [just] speak a word, and my servant boy **will be
healed**"... Now when Jesus heard this, He marveled at
him, and He turned and said to the crowd that followed
Him, "I tell you, not even in [all] Israel have I found such
great faith [as this]." And when the messengers...returned
to the house, they found the bond servant *who had been ill*
quite well again. *{The centurion was declaring his faith.}*

Luke 7:7b, 9, 10 AMP

So we take comfort *and* are encouraged *and* confidently
and boldly **say,** "The Lord is my Helper; I will not be
seized with alarm [I will not fear or dread or be terrified]."
{Boldly speak out your faith in the Lord, your Helper.}

Hebrews 13:6a AMP

That in every thing ye are enriched by Him, in **all**
utterance, and in all knowledge.

1 Corinthians 1:5

170

And the inhabitant shall **not** **say**, "I am sick": the people that dwell therein shall be forgiven their iniquity.

Isaiah 33:24

"Let the weak **say**, 'I am strong.'" *{And in like manner, let the sick say, "I am well." Do not go by the circumstances!}*

Joel 3:10b

"I Am So Weak!"

 *One man came forward for prayer, explaining how weak he was. He said, "I am just so weak. I am so weak!" I told him to put Scripture in his mouth by saying, "I am strong in the Lord and in the power of His might!" He spoke it feebly. I encouraged him to say it over and over and to put his faith in what he was saying. I left him speaking while I prayed for others. After about ten minutes, he came up to me with a big grin on his face, flexing his muscles and saying, "I feel so strong! I feel so strong!" The effect of God's powerful Word was evident in his countenance and in his voice!*

I shall not die, but live, and <u>declare</u> the works of the LORD.

Psalm 118:17

Hold fast the form of sound words, which thou hast heard of me, in faith and love which is in Christ Jesus. *{This means, "Hold fast the pattern of <u>healthy</u>, <u>well</u>, uncorrupt, <u>whole(some)</u> **words**, which thou hast heard of me... (from Strong's Concordance, word 5198 "sound"). }*

2 Timothy 1:13

"I create the **fruit** of the lips," saith the LORD, "...and I will heal him."

Isaiah 57:19

...The Word is nigh thee, even in thy **mouth**, and in thy heart: that is, the Word of **faith**, which we preach.

Romans 10:8

"But the Word is very near you, in your **mouth** and in your mind *and* in your heart, so that you can do it." *{God's Word is <u>power!</u>}*

Deuteronomy 30:14 AMP

And I heard a loud voice saying in heaven, "Now is come salvation *{<u>health</u>, deliverance, rescue, safety}*, and strength, and the kingdom of our God, and the power of His Christ: for the accuser of our brethren is cast down, which accused them before our God day and night. And they overcame him by the blood of the Lamb, and by the **word of their testimony**..."

Revelations 12:10, 11

WARNINGS

Some Ways Healing Can Be Missed

... Of a truth I perceive that God is no respecter of persons.

"My people are destroyed for <u>lack of knowledge</u>."

Hosea 4:6a

And He replied to them, "To you it has been given to <u>know</u> the secrets *and* mysteries of the kingdom of heaven, but to them it has not been given. For this nation's heart has grown gross (fat and dull), and their ears heavy *and* difficult of hearing, and their eyes they have tightly closed, lest they see *and* perceive with their eyes, and hear *and* comprehend the sense with their ears, and grasp *and* understand with their heart, and turn *and* I should heal them." [Isa. 6:9,10.] *{We can know the secret of health. Jesus is waiting for us to understand, so that He may heal us.}*

Matthew 13:11, 15 AMP

Therefore they <u>could not</u> believe. For Isaiah has also said: "He (Satan) has blinded their eyes and hardened and benumbed their [callous, degenerated] hearts to keep them from seeing with their eyes and understanding with their hearts and minds and repenting and turning to Me to heal them." [Isaiah 6:9, 10]

John 12:40 AMP

"...I have set before you life and death, blessing and cursing: therefore **choose** <u>life</u>, that both thou and thy seed may live:" *{We make the choice.}*

Deuteronomy 30:19

"As for what was sown among thorns, this is he who hears the Word, but the cares of the world and pleasure *and* delight *and* glamour *and* deceitfulness of riches choke *and* suffocate the Word, and it yields no fruit." *{Do not let worry and the distractions of the world cause God's Word to become unfruitful in your life.}*

Matthew 13:22 AMP

Thou hast neither part nor lot in this matter: for thy heart is not right in the sight of God. *{If your heart is not right towards healing, you will have no part in this blessing of God.}*

Acts 8:21

Know ye not, that to whom ye yield yourselves servants to obey, his servants ye are to whom ye obey; whether of sin unto death, or of obedience unto righteousness? *{When we choose not to believe God's Word, we are believing the devil and not obeying God.}*

Romans 6:16

And He said unto them, "Full well ye reject the commandment of God, that ye may keep your own tradition...making the Word of God of none effect through your tradition..." *{We make God's Word ineffective when we reject His Words of Truth.}*

Mark 7:9, 13

"That's 20 Minutes Faster Than Advil!"

"I was over at the Insley's house and complained about having a headache. Nancy offered to pray for me, but I told her I would go home and take an aspirin, instead. She and her husband kept trying to convince me to receive prayer. I finally consented and was amazed. As soon as she prayed for me, all of the pain was gone. I exclaimed, 'Whoa! Wow! That's great! That's 20 minutes faster than Advil!'"—Mike, age 16

"A good man out of the good treasure of his heart bringeth forth that which is good; and an evil man out of the evil treasure of his heart bringeth forth that which is evil: for of the abundance of the heart his mouth speaketh." *{Is the abundance of your heart speaking faith and healing or doubt and sickness?}*

Luke 6:45

Take heed, brethren, lest there be in any of you an evil heart of **unbelief,**

Hebrews 3:12a

And some <u>believed</u> the things which were spoken, and some <u>believed not</u>. And when they agreed not among themselves, they departed, after that Paul had spoken one word, "Well spake the Holy Ghost by Esaias the prophet unto our fathers, saying, 'Go unto this people, and say, "Hearing ye shall hear, and shall not understand; and seeing ye shall see, and not perceive."

"'For the heart of this people is waxed gross, and their ears are dull of hearing, and their eyes have they closed; lest they should see with their eyes, and hear with their ears, and understand with their heart, and should be converted, and I should heal them.'"

Acts 28:24-27

Then Saul, (who also is called Paul,) filled with the Holy Ghost, set his eyes on him, and said, "O full of all subtilty and all mischief, thou child of the devil, thou enemy of all righteousness, wilt thou not cease to pervert the right ways of the Lord?" *{The devil uses people to pervert the Word of Truth about healing, the baptism of the Holy Spirit, the present-day validity of the gifts of the Holy Spirit and more.}*

Acts 13:9, 10

...I Nebuchadnezzar lifted up mine eyes unto heaven, and mine understanding returned unto me... *{When our eyes remain fixed on God and not on the circumstances, our understanding of Truth returns to us.}*

Daniel 4:34

Only do not rebel against the Lord... *{nor against His Word.}*

Numbers 14:9a AMP

The foolishness of man subverts his way [ruins his affairs]; then his heart is resentful *and* frets against the Lord. *{It is foolish to speak what does not agree with the Word of the Lord. People speak sickness, disease and negative doctors' reports and then become resentful against God for not healing them—but they have subverted their <u>own</u> way!}*

Proverbs 19:3 AMP

Some are fools [made ill] because of the way of their transgressions and are afflicted because of their iniquities.

Psalm 107:17 AMP

If I regard iniquity in my heart, the Lord will not hear me; but certainly God has heard me; He has given heed to the voice of my prayer. Blessed be God, Who has not rejected my prayer nor removed His mercy *and* loving-kindness from being [as it always is] with me.

Psalm 66:18-20 AMP

Now the works of the flesh are manifest, which are these; Adultery, fornication, uncleanness, lasciviousness, idolatry, witchcraft, hatred, variance, emulations, wrath, strife, seditions, heresies, envyings, murders, drunkenness, revellings, and such like: of the which I tell you before, as I have also told you in time past, that they which do such things shall not inherit the kingdom of God. *{These things can also hinder a Christian from receiving the promises of God.}*

Galatians 5:19-21

Be not deceived; God is not mocked: for whatsoever a man soweth, that shall he also reap. *{Don't sow sickness with your words, actions and expectations; sow health.}*

Galatians 6:7

Curse not the king, no not in thy thought *{Even our thoughts must be pure, and they must line up with the Word of God.}*

Ecclesiastes 10:20a

Casting down imaginations, and every high thing that exalteth itself against the knowledge of God, and bringing into captivity every thought to the obedience of Christ; *{This is an extremely important verse for attaining victory in any area of your life. Do not allow yourself to entertain thoughts that go against the Word of God—like thoughts of* *sickness. Take such thoughts captive. Replace them with healing Scriptures. What you focus on will determine your attitude, your behavior and your actions.}*

2 Corinthians 10:5

Riddled With Cancer

I have seen a large number of people healed who were dying of cancer. To God, healing cancer is no different from any other healing. I have been sent to folks whose bodies were riddled with cancer, on hospice, just waiting to die. God has taken the symptoms and healed all of them. Every cancerous cell has been restored. Doctors have confirmed that they cannot find a single cancerous cell in the patients' bodies.

Sometimes a prayer cloth is sent to the person with cancer, or I pray with them over the phone. Cancer has disappeared with each of these methods. Do not lose faith. We serve a mighty God!

{Jacob made an agreement with his father-in-law Laban for his hire.} "Let me pass through all your flock today, removing from there all the speckled and spotted sheep, and all the brown ones among the lambs, and the spotted and speckled among the goats; and these shall be my wages. So my righteousness will answer for me in time to come, when the subject of my wages comes before you: every one that is not speckled and spotted among the goats, and brown among the lambs, will be considered stolen, if it is with me."

Now Jacob took for himself rods of green poplar and of the almond and chestnut trees, peeled white strips in them, and exposed the white which was in the rods. And the rods

which he had peeled, he set before the flocks in the gutters, in the watering troughs where the flocks came to drink, so that they should conceive when they came to drink. So the flocks conceived before the rods, and the flocks brought forth streaked, speckled, and spotted.
And it came to pass, whenever the stronger livestock conceived, that Jacob placed the rods before the eyes of the livestock in the gutters, that they might conceive among the rods. But when the flocks were feeble, he did not put them in; so the feebler were Laban's and the stronger Jacob's. *{Those flocks birthed what they focused on! This was supernatural, but so is healing. What you focus on and give attention to, you will give birth to. What are the thoughts of your heart pertaining to healing?}*
Genesis 30:32, 33, 37-39, 41, 42 NKJV

For the thing which I greatly **feared** is come upon me, and that which I was afraid of is come unto me. *{Fear was Job's open door, allowing an entrance for the devil. If we are ignorant of the devil's wiles, we can be tricked and plagued through similar open doors.}*
Job 3:25

The thing a wicked man **fears** shall come upon him, but the desire of the [uncompromisingly] righteous shall be granted.
Proverbs 10:24 AMP

Be still *and* rest in the Lord; wait for Him *and* patiently lean yourself upon Him; fret not yourself...
Psalm 37:7 AMP

Be strong and let your heart take courage, all you who wait for *and* hope for *and* expect the Lord!
Psalm 31:24 AMP

Do not fret *or* have any anxiety about anything, but in every circumstance *and* in everything, by prayer and petition (definite requests), with thanksgiving, continue to make your wants known to God. And God's peace...which transcends all understanding shall garrison *and* mount guard over your hearts and minds in Christ Jesus.
Philippians 4:6, 7 AMP

"<u>If</u> ye keep My commandments, ye shall abide in My love... These things have I spoken unto you, that My joy might remain in you, and that your joy might be full."
John 15:10, 11

Finally, brethren, whatsoever things are true, whatsoever things are honest, whatsoever things are just, whatsoever things are pure, whatsoever things are lovely, whatsoever things are of good report; if there be any virtue, and if there be any praise, think on these things. *{Do <u>not</u> think on illness. What you think on is key to what you will receive.}*
Philippians 4:8

And set your minds *and* keep them set on what is above (the higher things), not on the things that are on the earth.
Colossians 3:2 AMP

Meditate upon these things; give thyself wholly to them; that thy profiting may appear to all. Take heed unto thyself, and unto the doctrine; continue in them: for in doing this thou shalt both save *{sozo}* thyself, and them that hear thee. *{One of the meanings of "sozo" is "to heal". As we stay focused on God's Truth, we will be healed.}*
1 Timothy 4:15, 16

For as he thinketh in his heart, so is he... *{If you see yourself as sick, you shall remain so. No matter what words you speak out of your mind, you will <u>be</u> as you truly*

believe yourself to be in your heart. You must meditate on healing Scriptures until they are cemented in your spirit.}
Proverbs 23:7

A sound heart is the life of the flesh: but envy the rottenness of the bones. *{Envy causes sickness.}*
Proverbs 14:30

A calm *and* undisturbed mind *and* heart are the life *and* health of the body, but envy, jealousy, *and* wrath are like rottenness of the bones. *{Our minds are undisturbed when we stand in trusting faith.}*
Proverbs 14:30 AMP

All the days of the afflicted are evil *{grievous, misery}*: but he that is of a merry heart hath a continual feast.
Proverbs 15:15

A merry heart doeth good like a medicine: but a broken spirit drieth the bones. *{Drying of the bones could describe osteoporosis.}*
Proverbs 17:22

for the joy of the LORD is your strength.
Nehemiah 8:10b

Concerning the works of men, by the Word of Your lips I have avoided the ways of the violent (the paths of the destroyer).
Psalm 17:4 AMP

When I kept silence [before I confessed], my bones wasted away through my groaning all the day long. *{Unconfessed sin can make us ill.}*
Psalm 32:3 AMP

(When Jesus was being tempted, He responded:) "It is written, 'That man shall not live by bread alone, but by every **Word** of God.'" *{We can only truly <u>live</u> when we know, trust and respond to the Word of God.}*

Luke 4:4

No More Kidney Stones

One lady was in such pain from kidney stones that I was asked to go to her without delay. The pain instantly left her, and she was ecstatic. The symptoms of an earlier stroke also began disappearing immediately.

For many years, I also had a problem with kidney stones. Several years ago, I was healed of those and have had no issues with them since.

Blessed is the man that walketh not in the counsel of the ungodly, *{This could be the counsel of unbelieving doctors or counselors, instead of walking in the promises of God.}*

Psalm 1:1a

...nor standeth in the way of sinners, nor sitteth in the seat of the scornful. *{Many scorn this message of faith and healing.}*

Psalm 1:1b

But his delight is in the law of the LORD; and in His law doth he <u>meditate day and night</u>. And he shall be like a tree planted by the rivers of water, that bringeth forth his fruit in his season; his leaf also shall not wither; and whatsoever he doeth shall prosper. *{If you will delight in the promises of God and meditate therein day and night, you will flourish and prosper. Meditate on and speak His Word, and it will prosper in the thing whereto He sent It.}*

Psalm 1:2, 3

"This book of the law shall not depart out of thy mouth; but thou shalt meditate therein day and night, that thou mayest observe to do according to all that is written therein: for then thou shalt make thy way prosperous, and then thou shalt have good success."

Joshua 1:8

Behold, the LORD thy God hath set the land before thee: go up and possess it, as the LORD God of thy fathers hath said unto thee; "Fear not, neither be discouraged." *{Do not be discouraged or in fear. God's promises are ours to have.}*

Deuteronomy 1:21

O you who love the Lord, hate evil; He preserves the lives of His saints (the children of God), He delivers them out of the hand of the wicked.

Psalm 97:10 AMP

Be sober, be vigilant; because your adversary the devil, as a roaring lion, walketh about, seeking whom he may devour: Whom resist stedfast in the faith, knowing that the same afflictions are accomplished in your brethren that are in the world.

1 Peter 5:8, 9

(Anger, wrath:) Leave no [such] room *or* foothold for the devil [give no opportunity to him]. *{We are the ones who determine how much influence the devil will have in our lives.}*

Ephesians 4:27 AMP

That ye be not slothful, but followers of them who through faith and patience inherit the promises.

Hebrews 6:12

Do not, therefore, fling away your fearless confidence, for it carries a great *and* glorious compensation of reward. For you have need of steadfast patience *and* endurance, so that you may perform *and* **fully** accomplish the will of God, and thus receive *and* carry away [and enjoy to the full] what is promised. *{Do not give up; be steadfast.}*

Hebrews 10:35, 36 AMP

But let endurance *and* steadfastness *and* patience have full play *and* do a thorough work, so that you may be [people] perfectly and fully developed [with no defects], <u>lacking in nothing</u>.
Only it must be in **faith** that he asks with no wavering (no hesitating, no doubting). For the one who wavers (hesitates, doubts) is like the billowing surge out at sea that is blown hither *and* thither and tossed by the wind. For truly, let not such a person imagine that he will receive anything [he asks for] from the Lord.
[For being as he is] a man of <u>two minds</u> (hesitating, dubious, irresolute), [he is] unstable *and* unreliable *and* uncertain about everything [he thinks, feels, decides].

James 1:4, 6-8 AMP

(Lame man at pool:) Afterward when Jesus found him in the temple, He said to him, "See, you are well! Stop sinning or something worse may happen to you." *{Keep no doors opened to the devil!}*

John 5:14 AMP

Know ye not that your bodies are the members of Christ? ...What? know ye not that your body is the temple of the Holy Ghost which is in you, which ye have of God, and ye are not your own? For ye are bought with a price: therefore glorify God in your body, and in your spirit, which are God's. *{Deformed bodies—a result of our fallen world— can be made whole. God receives glory when bodies are healed, not when they are deformed or sickly. In the Old Testament, only unblemished animals were acceptable to God. Jesus, the perfect Lamb, was also without blemish.}*

1 Corinthians 6:15a, 19, 20

"Neither do men put new wine into old bottles: else the bottles break, and the wine runneth out, and the bottles perish: but they put new wine into new bottles, and both are preserved." *{We are new creations with the new wine of the Holy Spirit. We can now live a new life of health.}*

Matthew 9:17

God Heals Allergies, Too

A woman had an allergy which caused the backs of her hands to be extremely dry and covered with a rash. I prayed over her, but I did not see any results. I asked the Lord what He wanted me to do. He had me tell her to shake her hands, as if she were shaking off the sickness. She obeyed God's leading, acting on faith, and shook them. We looked down at her hands, and they were perfectly clear! There was no more rash, and her hands were no longer dry. She started dancing and singing and praising God.

The Spirit Himself [thus] testifies together with our own spirit, [assuring us] that we are children of God, And if we are [His] children, then we are [His] heirs also: heirs of God and fellow heirs with Christ [sharing His inheritance with Him]; only we must share His suffering if we are to share His glory. *{Jesus was suffering persecution, not sickness. We never are told that Jesus was ill. The word "suffer" in this verse means "to suffer with, specifically persecution" (Strong's Concordance, word 4841).}*

Romans 8:16, 17 AMP

{Oftentimes people refer to the thorn in Paul's side as being a sickness God was allowing or causing him to suffer. However, Paul himself made it quite clear that it

was persecution. Also, the source of the thorn is evident:} And lest I should be exalted above measure through the abundance of the revelations, there was given to me a thorn in the flesh, the messenger of Satan to buffet me, lest I should be exalted above measure. *{Buffeting is not sickness, but a hitting of the fists. According to Rick Renner in his book Sparkling Gems From the Greek, page 853, the Greek tense describes "unending, unrelenting, continuous, repetitious beatings." Compare also with Colossians 1:24, where Paul expresses that his suffering is for the sake of the Gospel (that is, not sickness).}*

2 Corinthians 12:7

{Compare the last verse to this one:} "But if ye will not drive out the inhabitants of the land from before you; then it shall come to pass, that those which ye let remain of them shall be pricks in your eyes, and thorns in your sides, and shall vex you in the land wherein ye dwell."

Numbers 33:55

{In these next two verses, God tells how the Canaanites would be thorns in the flesh of the Israelites:} ...they shall be snares and traps unto you, and scourges in your sides, and thorns in your eyes...

Joshua 23:13

"I will not drive them out from before you; but they shall be as thorns in your sides, and their gods shall be a snare unto you." *{Thorn means in the original "**prick**, point, or prickle". There is nothing mentioned of illness; it is certainly a nuisance or persecution, however. Think of the Gospel accounts of seeds being sown. Some fell among the thorns. The **thorns** sprang up and choked them. Here, again, it is the buffeting of Satan or his thorns that choke us and beat us down. Persecution came against Paul in an attempt to kill him and to prevent him from passing on to future generations the revelations he had received.}*

Judges 2:3

Let no corrupt communication proceed out of your mouth, but that which is good to the use of edifying, that it may minister grace unto the hearers. *{Words of sickness do not edify.}*

Ephesians 4:29

Let no one say when he is tempted, "I am tempted from God;" for God is incapable of being tempted by [what is] evil and He Himself tempts no one. *{God would never tempt nor try us with sickness.}*

James 1:13 AMP

"My Hip Never Hurt Like That Before!"

"I had always been skeptical about healing. I knew it existed, but I had never seen it, nor did I expect it for myself. I had had pain in my right hip for years. I tried physical therapy, acupuncture and exercise; but there was no significant improvement. One leg was shorter than the other, causing the hip to be out of alignment. As I listened to the teaching on healing, my hip began hurting more and more. When I stood up, I almost fell over! My hip had never hurt like that before! When prayer was offered and hands laid on my hips, I did not feel anything happen; however, when I pressed the area that always hurt to touch, there was no pain! There has now been no pain since that time eight months ago."—Jody L.

Neither murmur ye, as some of them also murmured, and were destroyed of the destroyer.

1 Corinthians 10:10

I have forgiven...to keep Satan from getting the advantage over us; for we are not ignorant of his wiles *and* intentions.

2 Corinthians 2:10b, 11 AMP

But wilt thou know, O vain man, that faith without works is dead?

James 2:20

[As you draw near to God] be deeply penitent and grieve, even weep [over your disloyalty]. *{Not truly trusting the Word of God is being disloyal to Him.}*

James 4:9a AMP

Therefore to him that knoweth to do good, and doeth it not, to him it is sin. *{It is good to agree with God and to speak His Word about healing. It is sin not to do so.}*

James 4:17

Thy Word have I hid in mine heart, that I might not sin against Thee.

Psalm 119:11

And said, "If thou wilt diligently hearken to the voice of the LORD thy God, and wilt do that which is right in His sight, and wilt give ear to His commandments, and keep all His statutes, I will put none of these diseases upon thee...for I am the LORD that **healeth** thee." *{When we are in His will, we are under His protection.}*

Exodus 15:26

Humble yourselves in the sight of the Lord, and He shall lift you up.

James 4:10

"Now the just shall live by **faith**: but if any man <u>draw back</u>, My soul shall have <u>no pleasure</u> in him."

Hebrews 10:38

For whatever does not originate *and* proceed from faith is sin [whatever is done without a conviction of its approval by God is sinful]. *{Complaining, talking the problem and lack of faith towards healing are sin.}*

Romans 14:23b AMP

So we take comfort *and* are encouraged *and* confidently *and* boldly say, "The Lord is my Helper; I will not be seized with alarm [I will not fear or dread or be terrified]. ..." *{Never fear pain, disease nor a doctor's report. Be comforted in knowing that the Helper will be faithful to His Word.}*

Hebrews 13:6 AMP

God is not a man, that He should lie; neither the son of man, that He should repent: hath He said, and shall He not do it? or hath He spoken, and shall He not make it good?

Numbers 23:19

...You do not have, because you do not ask. *{God is willing to answer our prayers.}*

James 4:2c AMP

Ye ask, and receive not, because ye ask amiss...

James 4:3

There is therefore now no condemnation to them which are in Christ Jesus, who walk not after the flesh, but after the Spirit. *{If you are walking after the flesh, agreeing with your flesh instead of agreeing with God's Word and His Spirit, you set yourself up for condemnation.}*

Romans 8:1

Trust in the LORD with all thine heart, and lean not unto thine own understanding. In **all** thy ways acknowledge Him, and He shall direct thy paths. Be not wise in thine own eyes: fear the LORD, and depart from evil. It shall be health to your navel *{body}*, and marrow *{refreshment or moistening}* to thy bones.

Proverbs 3:5-8

Has not God shown up the nonsense *and* the folly of this world's wisdom? *{We have been listening to the speech and "wisdom" of this world for too long. It is time to live according to the promises in God's Word!}*

1 Corinthians 1:20d AMP

My son, attend to my words; incline thine ear unto my sayings. Let them not depart from thine eyes; keep them in the midst of thine heart. For they are life unto those that find them, and **health** to all their flesh.

Proverbs 4:20-22

Toothaches Gone

In Madagascar, the Philippines, Croatia and the United States, many people have been instantly relieved of toothaches. One 13-year-old boy, who had been miserable, was very pleased when he was miraculously healed.

One woman was in such pain that she could not even open her jaw before she received prayer. She, too, was completely healed.

My son, let not them depart from thine eyes: keep sound wisdom and discretion: So shall they be life unto thy soul, and grace to thy neck. Then shalt thou walk in thy way safely, and thy foot shall not stumble.

Proverbs 3:21-23

For the time being no <u>discipline</u> brings joy, but seems grievous *and* painful; but afterwards it yields a peaceable fruit of righteousness to those who have been trained by it [a harvest of fruit which consists in righteousness—in <u>conformity to God's will</u> in purpose, thought, and action, resulting in right living and right standing with God]. So then, brace up *and* reinvigorate *and* <u>set right</u> your slackened *and* weakened *and* drooping hands and strengthen your feeble *and* palsied *and* tottering knees, [Isa. 35:3.] And cut through *and* make firm *and* plain *and* smooth, <u>straight paths</u> for your feet [yes, make them safe and upright and happy paths that go in the right direction], so that the lame *and* halting [limbs] may <u>not</u> be put out of joint, but rather may be **cured.** *{In order to conform to the will of God (for example, walking in health), we must be disciplined.}*

Hebrews 12:11-13 AMP

Correction is grievous unto him that forsaketh the way: and he that hateth reproof shall die.

Proverbs 15:10

{Many verses talk about God's will for us to live a <u>long life</u>, but <u>we greatly influence what determines the length of our days</u>. In addition to the following printed verses, please also read Deuteronomy 4:40, Deuteronomy 11:9 and 21, Deuteronomy 22:7, Psalm 34:12-14, Proverbs 3:13 with verse 16, Genesis 20:7, 1 Samuel 2:29 and 33, Psalm 90:10, Genesis 15:15 and Job 5:26.}

Honour thy father and mother; (which is the first commandment with promise;) That it may be well with thee, and thou mayest live long on the earth.

Ephesians 6:2, 3

The prince that wanteth *[lacks]* understanding is also a great oppressor: but he that hateth covetousness shall prolong his days.

Proverbs 28:16

The fear of the LORD prolongeth days: but the years of the wicked shall be shortened.

Proverbs 10:27

Be not over much *[exceedingly]* wicked, neither be thou foolish: why shouldest thou die <u>before thy time</u>?

Ecclesiastes 7:17

Wherefore whosoever shall eat this bread, and drink this cup of the Lord, unworthily, shall be guilty of the body and blood of the Lord. But let a man examine himself, and so let him eat of that bread, and drink of that cup. For he that eateth and drinketh unworthily, eateth and drinketh damnation to himself, not discerning the Lord's body. For this cause many are <u>weak</u> and <u>sickly</u> among you, and many sleep *[<u>die</u>]*.

1 Corinthians 11:27-30

He taught me also, and said unto me, "Let thine heart retain my words: keep my commandments, and live."

Proverbs 4:4

My son, forget not my law; but let thine heart keep my commandments: For length of days, and long life, and peace, shall they add to thee.

Proverbs 3:1, 2

Hear, O my son, and receive my sayings; and the years of thy life shall be many.

Proverbs 4:10

Ye shall walk in all the ways which the LORD your God hath commanded you, that ye may live, and that it may be well with you, and that ye may <u>prolong</u> your days in the land which ye shall possess.

Deuteronomy 5:33

That thou mightest fear the LORD thy God, to keep all His statutes and His commandments, which I command thee, thou, and thy son, and thy son's son, all the days of thy life; and that thy days may be <u>prolonged</u>.

Deuteronomy 6:2

CONCLUSION

God wants only good things for us. Deuteronomy 28:1-14 lists the blessings He desires for us: "And it shall come to pass, if thou shalt hearken diligently unto the voice of the LORD thy God, to observe and to do all His commandments which I command thee this day, that the LORD thy God will set thee on high above all nations of the earth: And **all** these blessings shall come on thee, and overtake thee, if thou shalt hearken unto the voice of the LORD thy God" (verses 1-2). Not one single letter of His law will fail (Luke 16:17). If we follow His Word, the blessings will overtake us; if we go a different direction and step outside of His covering, the devil can wreak havoc in our lives. However, we have authority over the works of the enemy, we have been redeemed from all curses, and as "we confess our sins, He is faithful and just to forgive us our sins" (1 John 1:9). Regardless of where we stand with God or what we might have done, we can always reestablish our right relationship with the Lord.

My prayer for you is "(t)hat the God of our Lord Jesus Christ, the Father of glory, may give unto you the spirit of wisdom and revelation in the knowledge of Him: The eyes of your understanding being enlightened; that ye may know what is the hope of His calling, and what the riches of the glory of His inheritance in the saints, and what is the exceeding greatness of His power to us-ward who believe, according to the working of His mighty power, which He wrought in Christ, when He raised Him from the dead, and set Him at His own right hand in the heavenly places, far above **all** principality, and power, and might, and dominion, and every name that is named, not only in this world, but also in that which is to come: And hath put <u>all</u> things under His feet, and gave Him to be the head over all things to the church, which is His body, the fulness of Him that filleth all in all" (Ephesians 1:17-23).

Because God is no respecter of persons (Romans 2:11), He would not choose to heal some but not others. He has proven over and over again that He wants to heal us **all**. "For what if some did not believe? Shall their unbelief make the faith of God without effect?" (Romans 3:3). No. "...the Word preached did not profit them, not being mixed with faith in them that heard it" (Hebrews 4:2). Mix faith with what you have now heard.

"Therefore it is of <u>faith,</u> that it might be by grace, to the end the promise might be sure to all the seed" (Romans 4:16a). "Whereby are given unto us exceeding great and precious promises: that by these ye might be partakers of the divine nature" (2 Peter 1:4a). By partaking of His great promises, we can live the divine nature, which includes divine health.

How did you get saved? You heard the Gospel and believed. That was exercising faith. It is just as simple to be healed. You have now heard the Word and believe. Receive your healing. A lack of faith comes from a lack of knowing God's Word: God said, "My people are destroyed for lack of knowledge" (Hosea 4:6a); but you are no longer ignorant of His Word and His promises. "Study (be prompt, be earnest, be diligent, endeavor) to shew thyself approved unto God, a workman that needeth not to be ashamed, rightly dividing the Word of Truth" (2 Timothy 2:15). I thank God, "because, when ye received the Word of God which ye heard of me, ye received it not as the word of men, but as it is in Truth, the Word of God, which effectually worketh also in you that believe" (1 Thessalonians 2:13).

May "the Word of Christ dwell in you richly in all wisdom" (Colossians 3:16a). "And why call ye Me, Lord, Lord, and do not the things which I say?" (Luke 6:46). "But be doers of the Word [obey the message], and not merely listeners to it, betraying yourselves [into deception by reasoning contrary to the Truth]" (James 1:22 AMP). "For laying aside the commandment of God, ye hold the tradition of men" (Mark 7:8a). Do not listen to the doubt and lies of men (Satan's deception), but hold fast to God's promises. Do not let the teachings of man get in the way of your healing. Take authority over a spirit of fear, deception and error, and let God's Word and His Holy Spirit, which "shall teach you all things" (see John 14:26), minister to you. Say, "I have chosen the way of Truth" (Psalm 119:30a). WORSHIP GOD FIRST, then abiding in Him and with His Words abiding in you, make your requests known unto Him.

Jesus said that the prince of this world has no hold on Him. In John 14:20, it says that we are in Him and He is in us, so the destroyer also has no hold on us. It is not enough just to believe; we must confess the Word with our mouths (Romans 10:9), as is clearly shown in Mark 11:23 and in another way in Hebrews 4:14: "...let us hold fast our profession." We must constantly be "casting down imaginations, and every high thing that exalteth itself against the knowledge of God, and bringing into captivity every thought to the obedience of Christ" (2 Corinthians 10:5).

Because you will reap what you sow, sow healing verses; sow salvation verses; sow victorious, overcoming verses. Don't sow doubt and unbelief but faith. Our words carry power, either positive or negative. Base your petitions on God's Word, then stand on His Truth! God is great; God is good! Concentrate on loving God, then rest in Him. Psalm 22:3 states that God inhabits the praises of His people. Praise Him; worship Him.

God is our Source, our Provider and our Healer. We will always be healed through His Word. "My son, attend to my Words; incline thine ear unto my sayings. Let them not depart from thine eyes; keep them in the midst of thine heart. For they are **life** unto those that find them, and **health** to **all** their flesh" (Proverbs 4:20-22). God's Word is a healing agent. Take it according to the directions given. The Word is not a respecter of persons and will work for all who take it. Be able to say, "Thy Word have I hid in mine heart, that I might not sin against Thee" (Psalm 119:11). "For whatsoever things were written aforetime were written for our learning, that we through patience and comfort of the Scriptures might have hope (confident expectation)" (Romans 15:4). It is not a matter of whether God's Word works, but are you trusting and applying God's Word? See yourself healed.

When we are speaking and thinking of God and giving Him glory (instead of complaining about how successful Satan is), He is writing it down: "Then they that feared the LORD spake often one to another: and the LORD hearkened, and heard it, and a book of remembrance was written before Him for them that feared the LORD, and that thought upon His Name" (Malachi 3:16).

When Jesus "saw the throngs, He was moved with pity *and* sympathy for them, because they were bewildered (harassed and distressed and dejected and helpless), like sheep without a shepherd. [Zechariah 10:2.] Then He said

198

to His disciples, 'The harvest is indeed plentiful, but the laborers are few. So pray to the Lord of the harvest to force out *and* thrust laborers into His harvest'" (Matthew 9:36-38 AMP). We are those laborers being thrust out with His Truth into His harvest field. We carry the message and Truth of healing for the "throngs" still needing to hear it.

"In conclusion, be strong in the Lord [be empowered through your union with Him]; draw your strength from Him [that strength which His boundless might provides]" (Ephesians 6:10 AMP). "(T)hanks be to God, Who gives us the victory [making us conquerors] through our Lord Jesus Christ" (1 Corinthians 15:57 AMP)!

"The LORD liveth; and blessed be my Rock; and let the God of my salvation be exalted!" (Psalm 18:46). "Be exalted, O God, above the heavens! Let Your glory be over all the earth!" (Psalm 57:5 AMP). Amen and amen!

A PRAYER OF SALVATION

If you do not yet know this Jesus Who, through His great love, sacrificed Himself for you, I would like you to say the following prayer. After you have said it from your heart, you will be a part of God's family, and all of these promises you've been reading about in this book will be yours to claim.

Please pray this: "Heavenly Father, I come to You in the Name of Jesus. I know that You will receive me, because Your Word says, '...the one who comes to Me I will most certainly not cast out [I will never, no never, reject one of them who comes to Me]' (John 6:37 AMP). Thank You for that.

"Please forgive me for all my sin. Jesus, I believe that You are the Son of God, and that You died and rose again for me. Thank You for dying for me. I confess You as my Lord and Savior. Romans 10:13 says that whoever calls upon Your Name shall be saved. Lord, I call upon You now, and I commit my life to You—all that I am. You are now the Lord of my life.

"Your Word also says that '...with the heart man believeth unto righteousness; and with the mouth confession is made unto salvation' (Romans 10:10). Lord, I believe with my heart, and I confess You as my Lord, so now I am saved. I also receive from You the baptism of the Holy Spirit, with the evidence of speaking in a holy prayer language. Thank You, Father!"

You may now start a new life! Second Corinthians 5:17 says that you are a new creation (this means your spirit has been made alive in Christ), and that the "...old things are passed away, behold, all things are become new." The past is behind you, and you can start over as if you had never done anything wrong. Forget the pain and hurts of the past, and step into all that God has prepared for you by spending time with Him and in His Word. He has a future and a hope for you (Jeremiah 29:11). Congratulations, and welcome into the family of God!

APPENDIX

More Testimonies for Your Encouragement

In one two-week period of normal, daily life, I experienced over fifty healings! Who can say that God is not still working miracles?!?

For your encouragement, I want to share a few more healing testimonies with you.

Organs

One woman had been seeing a doctor, who was unable to determine the cause of her great pain, other than to say that it was possibly a problem in her liver, her gall bladder or her kidneys. He was also unable to help relieve or to alleviate the pain. A few days after receiving prayer, she wrote, "Not only is the pain gone, but the results of my CT scan were good this week. The physician said that there were no signs of cancer, scar tissue or gall stones!" God is truly our Healer!

Cancer and Growths

One lady brought her friend to my Bible study. She had been in the advanced stages of breast cancer. The cancer had spread throughout her body and was wrapped around her aorta, so the doctors were hesitant to operate. She was having pre-chemotherapy treatments. After prayer, she removed her nausea patch. She was able to sleep that night for the first time since her ordeal had begun. She found that she had no more need for pain medication for her head, her spine or her hip. When pain attacks came in the night, she would sit up, swing her legs over the edge of the bed, praise God and take authority over the pain. Then she would go right back to sleep. Three days after the prayer, she went to the doctor and requested that they re-test for cancer. The rating just two weeks before had been 73; that day it was only 15! Hallelujah!

A woman had a five-inch tumor on her spine, which had gradually spread up her entire spinal column. After receiving a prayer cloth and a copy of this book, she was able to stop all pain medication and enjoy her healing.

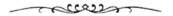

I was invited to go to a church to teach about healing. They had a gentleman who was terminally ill with lung cancer. The doctors had told him that his days were numbered, and that he should go home to get his affairs in order. His lungs, which were working at only 38% of capacity, were steadily deteriorating.

After prayer, I had him take several deep breaths. He instantly noted that he was able to breathe without *conscious effort. Color came back into his face, and his countenance began to change. I encouraged him to take a really deep breath—like he meant it. When he did that, a huge smile crossed his face. He was astounded at how easily he could breathe! I had him walk around, taking deep breaths. He said that he had not even been able to <u>walk</u> the day before. He said, "This is so exciting...but calming!"*

Multiple Sclerosis

A man had had multiple sclerosis for 20 years, and it was in a very advanced stage. The day we prayed for him, he had just run out of three of his medications. One of them was to combat the excruciating pain of a facial nerve that plagues victims of multiple sclerosis in its advanced stages. The end of the facial nerve splits or "explodes". It is so painful, that many will have the nerve severed, but this causes the face on that side to sag. Previously, if he went twenty-four hours without the medication, he was beside himself with pain. After learning about biblical healing and receiving prayer, he took no more medication and experienced no more pain! He was able to save $800 each month by not having to buy that one medication!

His wife had had lung issues since the time she had lost one lobe to cancer. She also suffered from many other ailments. A few days after prayer, she reported that her lungs, the ulcer, the problems with the digestive system and all of the other ailments were healed!

Accident

Shortly after hearing the teaching on healing, a woman was pulling a new jar of mayonnaise off of the top shelf of her refrigerator. It slipped out of her hands and landed with the edge of the lid on her foot. Within seconds, the foot was black and blue and swollen. Her young daughter, who noticed that she was in great pain, came over and lightly brushed her lips on the foot to "kiss it and make it better". This caused the mother to scream out as streams of pain shot up her leg. Her husband, who had also heard the teaching, came over to her and prayed for just a minute. As soon as he finished praying, the pain was gone, and the swelling and discoloration had completely disappeared!

Fibromyalgia With Many Other Ailments

When P. came to my house, she had about twelve different illnesses plaguing her, including fibromyalgia. She had also suffered multiple sensory deficit syndrome. As she listened to the Word on healing, she began to gain great understanding. She realized that she was claiming sickness, and that the more she talked about the sicknesses, the more her condition worsened. She also realized that she had gotten worse since joining a chat room of others with the same disease. She had begun to identify with their symptoms and to agree with their decisions—like staying at home, instead of going places. The more she listened to and identified with these others, the more ill she became. She also noticed an increase of odd sicknesses attacking her children. She recognized that there was a spirit of infirmity at work.

Because of past experiences where people were handling spiritual authority and the claiming of the Word irresponsibly, she was hesitant to step out in both of these areas. I was able to show her where the Word is very clear about these things. (We must know the Word of God well, so that we can recognize Truth and what deviates from the Word.)

*If Jesus says in Luke 10:19 that He has given us power over **all** the works of the enemy, and that **nothing** shall by any means hurt us, then that is true. Just because people exercise their authority inappropriately does not make the Word of God invalid. Abide in the Word, and look to Jesus as your example.*

The Holy Spirit kept revealing things to her, and she could see clearly in many areas why things were going awry. She could easily pinpoint her misunderstandings and errors. Things that had been confusing to her were made clear. Her mind was being dramatically renewed with the washing of the water of the Word.

She realized (as so many do) that she had not really exercised faith at all; but when it was time for us to pray together, she was ready to earnestly believe. God performed many miracles in her life; she could feel immediate changes taking place in her body. Praise God!

She left my house, and (as she put it) for two days 'walked in a daze of amazement and awe' over what salvation had really provided for her.

Just a few days later, I spoke with her. Everything had improved after that prayer. Her coloring was better, and her countenance had changed. She had already been able to cut all of her medications in half. Migraines, pain, depression and troubles with her nerve endings had all disappeared. Her husband noted one evening, "Wow! I can tell you are feeling better!"

If symptoms tried to return, she took authority over them, and they immediately disappeared. God revealed to her, that for the last five years, her hope had really been in the doctors and their treatments and not in Him.

When she was at my house, she had also complained that thinking was hard, as if her brain were in a fog. She reported that even the fog had lifted.

P. had suffered from tremendous fear (without realizing how out-of-control it had gotten), but that, too, had completely left her. She testified that she was able to go into stores with no concern, and that she had even spent the night in a hotel at the beach without a single worry.

She stopped visiting the internet site, where she had empathized with others suffering from the same sickness. She recognized that as soon as she starting speaking the problem and getting confirmation from others, the sickness rapidly worsened.

The family took a vacation a couple of weeks after our talk. At their family cabin, unusual, odd things would happen each time they were there, but only to their personal family. On this trip, every time something would start to happen, they would pray and successfully come against it.

They started living in the authority which Jesus had provided. The husband had an itching foot that had bothered him for a long time. He took authority over it, and the itching stopped immediately. He was also able to completely stop taking anti-depressant medication!

P. said, "The most exciting thing is that the Spirit has come alive in me. I really mean it! Friends are saying, 'I haven't heard you sound this good in 20 years!'"

She reported this: "Everything has improved since you prayed for me. I was trying to tell the doctor this, but he didn't want to listen to me; however, he admitted that my color was better, and that there was light in my countenance. I told him that the migraines, the pain in my body, the depression, the fear, and the problems with the nerve endings were all gone."

She was gaining great victory over her words, as well. Her daughter had called to say that the blood work of P.'s ten-month-old granddaughter had revealed leukemia. As her daughter was panicking, P. assured her that the baby did not have leukemia and would be perfectly fine. She continued to stand in faith. The blood tests were repeated, and *NO* sickness was found! Praise the Lord!

HIV/AIDS

One young gentleman, who received prayer, had suffered from the HIV virus. After he had his blood checked again, the laboratory called him to say that he needed to come in to repeat the test. There seemed to be an error, so they wanted to re-do it. When he met with the doctor after the second test, the man was asked if he had been taking drugs against AIDS. The doctor was convinced that he must have been taking something, because the tests showed that he was in excellent health!

Muscular Dystrophy

One time, I received a call to go and pray for a woman given only one week to live. She was dying from the effects of an advanced case of muscular dystrophy and was on life support.

As I prayed about whether or not I was to travel the three hours to see her, the Lord reminded me of others who had been healed with prayer cloths. I had an inner witness that I was not to spend the time traveling, but to pray over a cloth to send with others who were going up to see her.

As I prayed over that cloth, I knew that I was to take authority adamantly! I also knew to pray that the woman would be alert and that her heart would be softened to receive Christ as her Savior.

That is precisely what took place. The woman, who had been semi-comatose for days, was alert and sitting up in her bed. Her heart was softened and ready to receive the Gospel. After receiving the Lord, there was a dramatic change in her countenance.

After applying the prayer cloth, the woman did not die but was able to have all of the life support apparatus removed! She was taken from the ICU unit and sent to rehabilitation to prepare to return to normal life!

Crohn's Disease

In Europe, a woman was suffering greatly from Crohn's disease and had been hospitalized for several days. I visited her and anointed a prayer cloth for her. As soon as we finished praying, she was transported to an examination room for more testing. She kept the prayer cloth on her belly. After a thorough examination, the doctors were surprised to find nothing wrong with her! The pain caused by the Crohn's disease was gone, and the accompanying infection was also disappearing.

I also prayed for a woman in Seattle with Crohn's disease. The miracle-working power of God healed her as well!

Limbs

Carpal Tunnel Syndrome
A man was scheduled to have surgery for carpal tunnel syndrome, because his hand was already numb. Immediately after prayer, feeling came back into that hand!

I have prayed for a number of people with this syndrome. Another man was in great pain, hardly able to use his hands and wrists. As soon as he was prayed for, his amazement was reflected on his face as he began to flex *his fingers and to bend his wrists with absolutely no more pain!*

Circulation
One gentleman had extreme trouble with blood circulation to his fingers and toes. He said that they always felt like they were freezing. We were shocked when we looked at his hands: His palms were a rosy red, but all ten of his fingers (as well as all ten toes) were absolutely white! After praying, the blood instantly began to fill his fingers and his toes, turning them, too, a nice rosy red.

Short Leg
A 10-year-old girl had one leg six inches shorter than the other. Her femur had stopped growing, and her knee was permanently bent. As I prayed, I could feel her knee straightening and her leg getting longer!

Joints
My own elbow was hurting so badly that I could not sleep. Finally I spoke to it and said, "Elbow, listen up. Who are you going to listen to...to the devil or to me? By His stripes you were healed! Who are you going to listen to...to the devil or to me?" The pain immediately stopped and I could sleep!

Others have had immobile shoulder, knee and finger joints immediately loosen up and move as God intended them to. As soon as they move what had previously been immobile, they acquire their healing.

Oozing Sore
One lady had a sore on her leg that had been oozing for months. It stopped immediately. Others have seen bleeding instantly stop or wounds suddenly disappear. God is a marvelous Healer!

Injured Knee
A 12-year-old neighbor boy was walking up the street limping. He had injured his knee. The inside of the leg had a large bruise, and the outside was badly scraped. I asked

if he wanted prayer. He said "yes" and knelt down in the middle of the street. After prayer, I had him stand up and start bending his knee. He was amazed that the pain was gone and his mobility was back. A couple of days later, he saw me outside and came running over to me. "Nancy! I woke up the next morning, and <u>all</u> the pain was gone," he exclaimed while lifting his pant leg to show me, "and even the bruise was gone!! It is a miracle!" He was also very grateful to be able to play in the basketball game he thought he would miss due to the injured knee!

Leg With Bolts and Screws
One young man had plates and bolts in his leg, which had loosened and begun protruding through the skin. They were causing him great pain, so he asked for prayer. They immediately moved back into proper position!

Back Pain

I heard a woman in the grocery store groaning with every step that she took as she passed by me. I asked the Lord if I could pray for her. He said that I could, so I followed after her. When I asked if she was okay, she stated that her back was "killing" her. I asked if I could pray with her, and she quickly answered, "Yes," reaching out for my hands. Instead of taking her hands, I prayed and put my hand on her back. Then I told her to move around. To her astonishment, all the pain and discomfort had left her!

Epstein Barr Virus, Hormonal Imbalance, Extreme Fatigue and Depression

"I was always an active and happy person, but about a month before I turned 17, I started to suffer from extreme fatigue. It was so bad that I only made it through two weeks of my junior year, when I had to drop out. I had

already missed five days of school and could hardly get out of bed. I spent the next year with symptoms not only of chronic fatigue due to a virus called Epstein Barr, but also with a whole whirlwind of hormonal problems. I hadn't had a menstrual period for two years. I started to have insulin problems, depression, anxiety, insomnia, brain fog, food allergies, confusion and weakness. I could not take care of myself. All I could do was watch TV and sleep. I felt helpless. I felt like I was a burden to my family with all of the care I needed, although I knew they loved me.

"A year later, my condition had slightly improved. I started my senior year, but I still had all the symptoms and a "million" pills to take everyday. I would miss two weeks at a time, with only a few "good" days in between. If I stayed up just a little too late or ate the wrong thing, I would quickly fall back into an almost catatonic emotional state for the next five days. Nothing was working—not even all the prayers and blessings of others.

"I was so very discouraged until I met Nancy. God led Nancy to my mom, knowing I needed to learn that being a child of God means that you are already healed and Satan cannot put sickness in your body when you have taken this to heart and believe it 100%. I had thought that I would carry the diagnosis of chronic fatigue and polycystic ovarian syndrome for the rest of my life, but Nancy assured me that I had authority over what the enemy was doing in my body, because Jesus had died on the cross for me. It took a little while for it to sink in that I could be instantly healed and never have another sick day; but here I am, 18 years old, and about two weeks  *after Nancy's insight and prayers: I feel like a normal teenager with tons of energy, joy, focus and no mood swings. I even accidentally ate something I was "allergic" to, and I was fine! (I know better than to test the Lord, but when I ate the gluten, I KNEW I was fine.) I AM HEALED!!!!!" —Chloe*

Note: About a week later, another woman came for prayer with the same diagnosis of polycystic ovarian syndrome. She, too, was having an insulin-insufficiency problem due to this, which was requiring her to take insulin. As we prayed, God showed both her and another person in a vision how the cysts were being "popped" and the healing was taking place!

With more healings each week, I could continue relating wonderful testimonies to you, but I trust that you can see that God, through His infinite Love, wants each of us to enjoy the good health He offers us in His gift of salvation through Christ Jesus.

INDEX

Index

Index

217

Index

Index

Index

Index

Testimonies

Index

Teaching CD's are also available from

His Healing Touch

To order CD's on topics such as

Healing

Receiving Healing

Hindrances to Healing

Authority and Faith

Hearing the Voice of God

The Importance of Our Words

Or other topics,

Please email:

His Healing Touch

HisHealingTouchMinistry@msn.com

CPSIA information can be obtained at www.ICGtesting.com
Printed in the USA
BVOW010452310512

291185BV00006B/4/P